FERRARI

Dennis Adler

MBI Publishing Company

*To Jeanne, for making every day of
my life seem important.*

First published in 1997 by MBI Publishing Company,
PO Box 1, 729 Prospect Avenue, Osceola, WI
54020-0001 USA

The information in this book is true and complete to
the best of our knowledge. All recommendations are
made without any guarantee on the part of the author
or Publisher, who also disclaim any liability incurred in
connection with the use of this data or specific details.

We recognize that some words, model names and
designations, for example, mentioned herein are the
property of the trademark holder. We use them for
identification purposes only. This is not an official
publication.

MBI Publishing Company books are also available at
discounts in bulk quantity for industrial or sales-
promotional use. For details write to Special Sales
Manager at Motorbooks International Wholesalers &
Distributors, 729 Prospect Avenue, PO Box 1,
Osceola, WI 54020-0001 USA.

Library of Congress Cataloging-in-Publication Data

Adler, Dennis.
    Ferrari / Dennis Adler.
        p.   cm. -- (Enthusiast color series)
    Includes index.
    ISBN 0-7603-0273-1 (pbk. : alk. paper)
    1. Ferrari automobile--History. I. Title. II. Series
TL215.F47A34   1997
629.222'2--dc21   97-2402

On the front cover: The Luigi Chinetti Jr.-conceived NART
(North American Racing Team) Spyder was based on the
275 GTB/4. This was the first production touring
Ferrari to employ the four-cam V-12.

On the frontispiece: The monstrous radiator air intakes in
the nose of Ferrari's awe-inspiring F50 supercar.

On the title page: Even Ferrari's startling F50 is hard-
pressed to outgun its predecessor, the F40.

On the back cover: The 166 MM Touring Barchetta was
Ferrari's first sports car designed for mass consumption.
Luigi Villoresi raced the car shown, later selling it to race
driver and Ferrari importer Luigi Chinetti.

Printed in China

Contents

	Acknowledgments	6
Forward	**The Road From Maranello**	7
Chapter One	**The Early Years**	
	Race Cars & Road Cars	8
Chapter Two	**Carrozzeria**	
	Ferrari and the Italian Ateliers	22
Chapter Three	**Grand Touring**	
	The Elegant Ferrari	38
Chapter Four	**Ferraris for All Seasons**	
	The Great Road Cars	52
Chapter Five	**Contemporary Ferraris**	
	Road Cars of the 1980s and 1990s	72
	Index	96

Acknowledgments

Ferraris are a passion. They are more, much more than an automobile. For half a century the cars with the yellow and black Cavallino Rampante emblem have represented the ultimate expression of speed and automotive sensuality. Over the years they have been compared with the curvaceousness of a woman's body, the muscular stature of an athlete, and the grace and speed of a thoroughbred. Ferraris have been the benchmark by which all other sports cars have been judged for nearly 50 years.

Within these pages we celebrate the Ferrari legend, that of the man and his machines and all that they have meant to sports car enthusiasts since the early postwar years, when Enzo Ferrari lent his name to the first 125 Sport in 1947.

Names, it seems, have always been a part of the Ferrari legend. The names of engineers such as Gioacchino Colombo and Aurelio Lampredi, designers Carlo Felice Bianchi Anderloni, Giovanni "Pinin" Farina, Sergio Scaglietti, and Mario and Gian Paolo Boano have become as much a part of Ferrari lore as the cars themselves. And lest we forget the greatest Ferraristi of all, the late Luigi Chinetti, without whose efforts there would likely be little, if anything, to write about today.

It is perhaps Ferrari owners who deserve the most credit for having sustained the marque these many years through their continued support of Ferrari and dedication to the restoration and preservation of the early cars. As an author, photographer, and Ferrari enthusiast, I owe a great deal of thanks to collectors such as Robert M. Lee, Skeets Dunn, Ron Pinto, Andy Cohen, William Noon and the staff at Symbolic Motor Car Company, Jerry J. Moore, Bruce Meyer, Tom Reddington, and the late Henry Haga all of whom through their devoted patronage to Ferrari were instrumental in the creation of this book.

If it were possible to write a second dedication, this book would be for my late friend and mentor Dean Batchelor, perhaps one of the greatest Ferrari enthusiasts and historians ever. It was Dean who instilled in me the understanding and respect for the eccentricities of Ferrari, both the man and the cars, and who introduced me many years ago to Sergio Pininfarina, the architect of Ferrari's greatest road cars.

In planning this book, it was decided to pursue the rarest Ferrari road cars, rather than the better-known models, and in so doing we were able to locate and photograph many original prototypes and first production cars, some seen here for the first time in color.

Ferraris are perhaps the most written about but most difficult to understand sports cars in automotive history. It is with great respect that I mention those authors who have wheeled down the path of confusion that leads from Modena's door, most notably the work of Antoine Prunet, who has made understanding Ferrari history a crusade; the late Hans Tanner, who with Doug Nye created the most comprehensive history of the marque ever written; and, of course, Dean Batchelor, whose excellent Ferrari books have become a standard reference the world over.

Additional research for this book came from the remarkable two-volume set, *Ferrari Catalog Raisonne*, published in Italy by Automobilia, and *Ferrari—Design of a Legend, The Official History and Catalog*, by Gianni Rogliatti, Sergio Pininfarina, and Valerio Moretti, published by Abbeville Press.

Others who have contributed to the content of this book include authors T. C. Browne, Denise McCluggage, and Henry Rasmussen. A special note of thanks is also due to Robert M. Lee, Scott Bergan, Skeets Dunn, Luigi Chinetti, Jr., Sergio Pininfarina, and Scott Grundfor for their contributions.

My thanks to one and all for taking part.

Dennis A. Adler, Pennsylvania

Foreword

Ferrari road cars. My first reaction is simply extraordinary. Fifty years of dreams, dedication, and passion. In the following pages you will be presented a tribute and review of a half century of Ferrari the man, the company, and the automobile. It is a story of people—people with a common bond to produce the best racing and performance cars possible.

Shortly after World War II, Enzo Ferrari had decided to build machine tools, much as he had during the war years. Dad [Luigi Chinetti, Sr.] quite naturally opposed this proposition, and in short order he had himself, my mother, and me in Modena on a very cold day in December 1946.

I particularly remember the cold in the buildings at our destination—the necessary frugality of the postwar years. Despite the cold, the decision was made to build road and race cars, provided Dad could supply the clients. He certainly did that, and soon had sold some 12 automobiles to old acquaintances. Some were for the road, and some were for the track. In the latter, he shared the driving tasks with his friends and clients.

Dad won the first endurance race for Ferrari, the 12 hours of Paris. This established Ferrari as an absolutely first-rate competition car. Ferrari's reputation was further solidified by Dad's victories at Le Mans, Spa, and Montlhéry, all events run in 1949. Racing success translated into road car sales.

Not only were the mechanicals race bred, but the stunning designs were the *avante garde* of the Paris, Geneva, and Turin motor shows. Indeed, Italian designers were firmly at the forefront when it came to high-performance automobiles. In short, the Ferrari had confirmed all of the initial aspirations of that small group of visionaries following their passions.

Passion is what makes Ferrari what it is. Ferrari was passionate; my father was passionate. And Modena was passionate, and remains so to this day. The thrill of seeing those early racing cars being tested on the roads around Modena certainly shaped and influenced my life as well.

Outings with Dad when he was trying out a new car were some of the greatest moments of my young life. I went out with many test drivers, Sanesi and Guidotto of Alfa Romeo, Bertocchi of Maserati, and later Michael Parkes of Ferrari. Each had a particular feeling for the car and brought to the end result their particular *imprimatur*.

I deeply regret not being able to bring those years back. Imagine creating those wonderful machines from a clean sheet of paper, choosing engineers like Colombo and Lampredi to design the engines and chassis, and then bringing in the coachbuilders of one's choice to execute one's sculpture.

I remember one June day in 1963 when Dad went to Marenello, along with Mr. Figoni and myself. Figoni was the designer of the beautiful prewar Delahayes and Talbot-Lagos. We were to pick up a 250 Competition short wheelbase coupe and take it to Le Mans over the road. Three in a short-wheelbase berlinetta is difficult at best, and I being the youngest, got the gearbox. Dad firmly believed that testing a car on the road and breaking it in properly were important stages in race car preparation.

Although somewhat biased, I can say that he was probably one of the finest of the *metteurs aux points* in the world. He could bring a car to the highest level of preparation prior to driving it in competition. During all of those 1,000 km, he never missed a shift and was absolutely smooth to a degree that I rarely saw, even in other test drivers—and at 62 years of age!

With the pressure of having to find the necessary funding to go racing, both Dad and Mr. Ferrari had to sell cars on a regular basis. It was with great reluctance that Ferrari acquiesced to building convertibles for the American market. Certainly there had been models called "America," and even "Superamerica," but none was like the California Spyder. It was hard for the factory to understand a convertible as a serious fast car. To them high speed, really high speed, was the domain of the closed car. The California was a wonderful success, and it was followed by the 275 NART Spyder.

For many, the 1960s and early 1970s were the absolute high watermark of the sport and GT automobile. I would certainly subscribe to that. I can still hear those wonderful 3.0-liter sport and GT cars at Sebring, Rheims, Daytona, and, of course, Le Mans- battles with Ford, Porsche, Matra, Alfa and the battles between the Rodriguez brothers, Phil Hill, Gurney, Gendebien, and all the other names.

I look back on the 50 years with great love and sentiment. Ferrari is a story of people and certainly the people of Modena. When I built some of the special NART cars when some six or eight years ago, and I struggled through the Modena winter, I could feel some small kinship with all the people greater than me in whose footsteps I plodded, struggling to bring a new idea to the road.

When people in town would say *"Buon lavoro!"* meaning "Good work!" that said it all: Ferrari and Modena.

Thank you both—Ferrari and Modena—and even greater thanks to my parents for giving me the opportunity to bear witness to these wonderful years.

Congratulations to Dennis Adler for capturing this colorful and productive time and place, and spirit, in this engrossing and beautifully produced book.

Buon Lavoro Ferrari!

Luigi Chinetti, Jr.

Chapter One

The Early Years
Race Cars and Road Cars

It would be difficult to travel anywhere in the world today where the name Ferrari is unknown. In the late 1940s and early 1950s, however, it meant little to anyone not keeping abreast of current events on the European motorsports scene. In Italy, Ferrari's name was already legendary. In 1939, Enzo Ferrari resigned from Alfa Romeo, ending a 20-year career with a company where, at various times, he had served as engineer, factory driver, and finally—through Scuderia Ferrari—the man behind Alfa Romeo's proud racing team.

For most men his age, resignation after so many years with one company would have been prelude to

retirement, but for the 47-year-old Enzo Anselmo Ferrari it was a reaffirmation of belief in his destiny. Rather than retiring on the laurels of his brilliant career with Alfa Romeo, Ferrari embarked upon a new adventure as an independent industrialist establishing a factory in Maranello. Ferrari later described his decision as proof that during his 20 years with Alfa Romeo, he had "not lived off reflected light, so to speak." Wrote Ferrari, "I wanted to show that the level of notoriety I had reached was a legitimate and hard earned outcome of my own hard work and of my own aptitudes." Indeed, the accomplishments that had made Scuderia Ferrari renowned throughout European racing circles would establish "Ferrari the auto maker" almost from the moment he opened his doors.

Ferrari established Auto Avio Costruzione and set himself to the task of supervising the design of a new race car. His first examples were commissioned in 1939 by renowned race driver Alberto Ascari and the Marchese Lotario Rangoni Machiavelli di Modena. Completed for the 1940 Grand Prix of Brescia (a replacement for the Mille Miglia that year), neither car bore the Ferrari logo or name. Part of Enzo's contract with Alfa Romeo required that he not build or race cars under his own name for four years. Thus his first

The car pictured, chassis number 0160 ED, was driven for Scuderia Ferrari in the 1952 Tour of Sicily by Piero Taruffi. The second Vignale Sports Racing Spyder built, 0160 ED bore the traditional styling used on most of the 2.7-liter cars, including the distinctive ovoid portholes cut into the front fenders. One of the most significant styling cues of the 225 S, the portholes were not part of the original design. They were added by Vignale following the Tour of Sicily to improve heat extraction from the engine compartment. At the same time, Vignale removed the car's running lights, and the round openings that had flanked the oval grille were converted to air intakes, creating a new, more aggressive front visage.

"... small, red, and ugly ..." That was the account one Italian newspaper gave of the first Ferrari. The model pictured, a 166 Spyder Corsa, is not too different in apperance from the 1947 model 125 sports car shown at Piacenza on May 11, 1947. If the shoe fits ...

production car was known simply as Model 815, indicating the number of cylinders and the engine capacity.

Ferrari's four-year, non-competition agreement with Alfa Romeo was comfortably fulfilled during World War II. By 1945, he was free to begin building cars, but by then Italy had lost the war and Ferrari had lost hope, resigning himself to manufacturing machine tools, the modest business which had kept his factory open throughout the war.

Had it not been for the intervention of one man, there might not have been a Ferrari legend. Luigi Chinetti, a prewar comrade, had worked with Ferrari at Alfa Romeo. On Christmas Eve 1946, the 45-year-old Italian race driver and automotive entrepreneur went to see Ferrari. He found him sitting alone in his cold dark office pondering his future, one that in the postwar economy held little promise for Ferrari as a manufacturer of machine tools. He

was at a crossroad, torn between an unfulfilling business and the need to return to that which gave him pleasure, the design and production of sports cars. Europe's postwar economy, however, would not support the kind of automotive business Ferrari had started in 1939.

Chinetti had spent the war years in the United States, becoming a citizen in 1946, before returning that December with his wife and son to visit France and Italy. He had an idea, one that compelled him to drive all the way from Paris to Modena on Christmas Eve. There was indeed a market for European sports cars, not in Europe, but in the United States. He told Ferrari of his plan. "Let's make automobiles," he said. "That is the one thing we are good at." Ferrari considered the idea, and spoke of hiring Gioacchino Colombo, another Alfa Romeo colleague, to develop engines. That night, Luigi Chinetti and Enzo Ferrari

Built on the 88.6-inch wheelbase of the 212, the 225 S was essentially the same layout except for the enlarged engine capacity. The Vignale Spyder body, however, gave this model far more prestige both on and off the race track.

laid the groundwork for the postwar revitalization of *Auto Avio Costruzione*, soon to become *Auto Costruzione Ferrari*.

In creating his first postwar sports cars, Ferrari reasoned that if Maseratis had 4-cylinder engines, Talbots had 6, Alfa Romeos 8, why not 12 then for Ferrari? It was a decision that historian Hans Tanner would later refer to as ". . . daring and farsighted."

May 11, 1947, was the first time a car bearing the Ferrari name appeared in public. Sports cars were prac-

A trio of 36DCF Weber carburetors delivered the air/fuel mix to the V-12 engine in the 225 Sport. With an 8.5:1 compression ratio, output was 210 hp at 7,200 rpm, discharged to the rear wheels via a five-speed gearbox integral with the engine. The capacity of the Colombo short-block was increased to 2,715cc by taking the bore out to 70 mm. While the engine remained basically Colombo, the roller-type cam followers introduced by Lampredi were used. Most engines also had the 12-intake-port heads.

Stabilimenti Farina produced the first Ferrari cabriolet (011 S) pictured here. This is one of the oldest known road cars, built in 1949, and was displayed at the Geneva Salon by Luigi Chinetti. Geneva was Ferrari's first showing outside Italy. Ferrari had little interest in road cars; it was Luigi Chinetti who convinced Il Commendatore (Enzo Ferrari) to consider the advantages of manufacturing both competition and road-going sports cars. The lines of the car were similar to other Stabilimenti Farina (and Pinin Farina) designs of the time, such as the Alfa Romeo 6C 2500, and were repeated again on the Simca Sport.

ticing for racing at Piacenza, and two versions of the Type 125S 1.5-liter sports car were shown, a simple, two-seat Spyder Corsa, later referred to in an Italian newspaper as "small, red, and ugly," and a roadster with full bodywork by Carrozzeria Touring Superleggera. The 125 S was powered by a 60-degree V-12 engine designed, as Ferrari had suggested, by Gioacchino Colombo.

By 1948, the Ferrari factory was producing a small number of 12-cylinder *competizione* models. One of the earliest examples to wear the yellow-and-black Cavallino Rampante emblem was the Type 166 Spyder Corsa, a simple, cycle-fendered vehicle very similar in appearance to the previous year's Type 125 S and 159 S. That any resemblance to a road car could be found surrounding an early Ferrari chassis was tribute to the Milanese firm of Touring Superleggera.

Convinced by Chinetti of the necessity to offer models with more cosmopolitan appeal to serve the

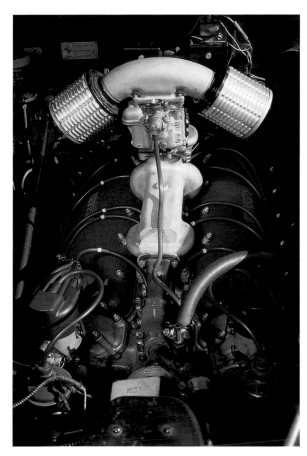

A single carburetor, a unique two-part air filter, and special covers unifying the ignition were characteristics of the first touring Ferraris. This is the original engine from the 166 Inter bodied by Stabilimenti Farina for the 1949 Geneva Salon.

All of the Barchetta bodies—of which Touring built some 46 examples—shared the same sleek, swept-back lines, long hood, short rear deck, and aggressively shaped oval grille, establishing this feature as a Ferrari trait for years to come. The Barchetta's visceral styling would also inspire the the AC Ace and other sports cars of the 1960s. In one bold stroke, Ferrari and Touring had ingeniously closed the distance between race car and road car, without compromising either. Sports cars would never be the same.

Designer Carlo Felice Bianchi Anderloni wrote that the styling of the Barchetta was both a fascinating and courageous undertaking, ". . . fascinating because we were attempting to individualize the Ferrari and not to copy one of the many 'Spider' two-seat sports cars in circulation. Courageous because the results were obtained by overturning the strictest canons of sports car design, which was normally wide at the bottom, narrow at the top and close to the ground." Conversely, the Barchetta had its maximum width just over halfway up the side and visibly high off the ground. It was so different from other sports cars, said Anderloni, that when journalists saw it on the Ferrari stand at the 1948 Turin Salon, they found it necessary to invent the name *Barchetta*, which literally means "small boat." Officially, the cars were cataloged as the 166 Mille Miglia, a name chosen in honor of Ferrari's 1948 victory in the grueling 1,000-mile Italian road race; however, Barchetta was readily used by everyone, even Ferrari.

The Touring design was not only revolutionary in form, utilizing the firm's exclusive "Superleggera" or "super-light" construction method of small, lightweight steel tubes to which the body panels were attached, but in its color scheme as well, sheathed in a unique blend of slightly metallicized red. Most of the 166 MMs were painted this color, which has become a Ferrari tradition. Virtually every Barchetta was a race car, whether *competizione*, powered by the 140-hp Export V-12, or *lusso*, with the 110-hp Inter V-12.

The 166 Mille Miglia was arguably the fastest sports car in the world at the time, and with it, Scuderia Ferrari's cannonade across Europe recorded more than 80 overall or class victories between April 1948 and December 1953.

needs of both road and track, Ferrari again retained Touring to create sports car bodies, this time to complement the unattractive but successful cycle-fendered Spyder Corsas that had become standard Ferrari fare. A year later, the first "sports car" design ever shown on a Ferrari chassis was introduced—the 166 Touring Barchetta. Few cars in automotive history have left such a lasting impression on the motoring world.

Almost 50 years after its debut, it is still considered among Ferrari's most admired models. The styling of the Barchetta was based in part on the BMW 328 Spyder, designed by Carrozzeria Touring in 1940.

Previous
The 166 Touring Barchetta was the first "sports car" design ever shown on a Ferrari chassis. The aggressive stance of the body was set atop the patented Superleggera welded tubular steel frame on a wheelbase of 86.6 inches. Track measured 49.8 inches front and 49.2 inches rear. The front suspension was Ferrari's independent A-arm design supported by a single transverse leaf spring. The rear utilized a live axle with semi-elliptic springs and parallel trailing arms on each side. Shock absorbers were the Houdaille hydraulic lever action type. The car pictured was originally raced by Luigi Villoresi and later sold to race driver and Ferrari importer Luigi Chinetti.

It was Chinetti who brought Ferrari its first significant postwar racing victory co-driving a 166 MM Touring Barchetta with Britain's Lord Peter Selsdon in the 1949 Vingt-Quatre Heures du Man. "Iron Man Chinetti" drove 23 of the 24 hours to clinch Ferrari's first and most important international win. Chinetti

Interior of the 166 Barchetta featured beautiful, hand-sewn leather upholstery and trim. Simplicity of design was purely race bred. The cars were considered luxe, or *lusso*, when given the full interior treatment. Note the five-speed shifter which has the gears lettered in Roman numerals.

went on to win the Spa-Francorchamps 24-hour race for touring cars the following July. In 1950, Alberto Ascari won the Grand Prix du Luxembourg and the Silverstone International Trophy. Dorino Serafini and Luigi Villoresi came in second at Silverstone driving a single-carburetor Barchetta, in all probability the very car pictured in this book, which was sold to Chinetti and later to American driver Bill Spear.

The differences between race car and road car were all matters of interpretation. The Barchetta was stunning but far from practical. It was strictly a fair-weather car. What Ferrari needed for the road was a convertible, and he turned to Stabilimenti Farina to build the first Ferrari cabriolet, chassis 011 S. The first convertible road car to wear the Ferrari badge made its debut at the 1949 Geneva Salon.

With the obvious exception of the roof, the convertible's design was almost identical to the 166 coupe, except for a flatter trunk, made necessary by the cabriolet top. The lines were simple and quite typical of Italian designs of the period. Aside from

The Colombo-designed 60-degree V-12 used in the 166 MM Touring Barchetta was as beautifully styled as the body surrounding it. With a displacement of 1,995cc (122ci), output was 140 hp at 6,600 rpm. A 60.0x58.8-mm bore and stroke (2.362x2.315 inches) and compression ratio of 10:1 were fueled by three Weber 32 DCF twin-choke, downdraft carburetors.

The 1951 Ferrari 212 was one of Maranello's first road cars. Many of the 212 bodies were produced by Carrozzeria Vignale and are considered among the most attractive of all early berlinettas. When the opportunity arose to build Ferrari's first noncompetitive model, Vignale and Michelotti penned designs that, while they may not have been altogether original, were executed to a level of quality few others were able to duplicate.

A hybrid combination of 212 Inter and Export, this luxurious Vignale coupe was equipped with the competition gas tank, fuel filler, and exposed spare but with the luxurious trim and upholstery of the noncompetition model. Chassis 175 E, it is believed, though not documented, competed in the 1951 Carrera PanAmericana.

By the early 1950s, Ferrari road cars were growing in number, and most of Italy's leading design houses were producing coachbuilt bodies to fit the new 212 Inter. Ferrari first turned to Carrozzeria Pinin Farina in 1952 to design a stylish sport cabriolet. The design, as would be expected from the avant-garde drafting board of Battista "Pinin" Farina, established a new styling trend with flat-sided body panels. The shape of many later sports car designs can be seen in this first Pinin Farina Ferrari.

the grille and bumpers, this first Ferrari cabriolet resembled the early postwar Alfa Romeo 6C 2500 Sport, designed by coachbuilder Pinin Farina, and the basic body lines of both cars were not too distant from those of the 1947 Cisitalia, also by Pinin Farina. The prototype cabriolet was purchased by Italian film director Roberto Rossellini.

One of the significant turning points in Ferrari road car production came in 1951, with the introduction of the Type 212. The 212 Berlinetta marked the beginning of a new era at Maranello. Where racing had once been Ferrari's sole *raison d'être*, the

design and production of *boulevardiers* had now taken on equal importance. Not everyone enthralled by illusions of the Ferrari's V-12 and exhilarating performance wanted to race, nor suffer the discomfort of a built race car's purpose-built interior and cockpit.

Although Ferrari considered competition his first priority, and had little, if any, interest in road cars, Chinetti convinced him that one could feed upon the other. Ferrari finally agreed with Chinetti's logic. The race cars improved the road cars, and the profits from their sales financed the development of race cars. Indeed, a competition engine could be

The 166 MM chassis were also fitted with a variety of coachbuilt designs by Italy's leading design houses, including a coupe by Allemano, an Inter coupe by Touring, an early berlinetta bodied by Stabilimenti Farina, and sport berlinettas produced by both Vignale and Touring Superleggera. The styling of the Touring Barchetta influenced this stunning berlinetta by Touring, produced in 1950. *Automobile Quarterly*

detuned for the street. And as for bodies, in postwar Italy, there was no shortage of coachmakers available to clothe the V-12's chassis. Bespoke coachwork from Italy's leading designers graced a number of early Ferrari chassis with exquisite two- and four-place creations such as Touring's 166 Inter coupe, the Ghia 212 Inter, and Pinin Farina's stunning Type 342 America of 1953.

Among the most stylish of early Ferrari road cars were those built by Vignale. The luxurious Vignale 212 Inter was intended as a touring car but also managed to do quite well when pressed into competition. A pair of 212 Inters finished first and second in the 1951 Carrera Panamericana, with Piero Taruffi and Luigi Chinetti in the lead car and Alberto Ascari and Luigi Villoresi close behind. The 212 could also be ordered in a stripped-down Export or *competizione* version. Even when built for racing, the Vignale was a car with striking *savoir-faire*. In all, it is estimated, and only estimated, since the assignment of serial numbers in the early years was less than precise, that around 80 Type 212 Inter (noncompetition models) were built and another 27 Exports (racing).

The 212 Inter's engine displaced 2,562.51cc (156.3ci), fueled by three Weber 36DCF carburetors. Output was rated at 180 hp at 7,000 rpm with 8:1 compression. (Some figures show 170 hp at 6,500 rpm.) Earlier engines had one 36 DCF Weber twin-choke carburetor and developed 130 hp at 6,000 rpm. The 60-degree V-12 was fitted with a light alloy cylinder head and block, special cast-iron pressed-in liners, an increased bore of 68 mm (2.68 inches), and the standardized stroke of 58.8mm (2.315 inches). Power was delivered via a five-speed non-synchromesh with direct drive in fourth gear.

As production of road cars progressed, interior treatments became more luxurious and the use of leather to cover door panels and the transmission tunnel more common. Aside from the instrument panel and the basic outline of the dashboard, interior decor was at the discretion of the individual coachbuilder and client.

The Vignale Inter represents the quintessence of the Italian coachbuilder's art in the 1950s. And it is here that the true romance of Ferrari's early years can be seen. There is so much handwork that one must study even the smallest appointments to appreciate the workmanship; hand-tooled door pulls with small Vignale cloisonnés; chromed window moldings and trimwork; hand-sewn leather and fabrics. In virtually every detail, inside and out, this was the work of artisans practicing skills that have long since been replaced by production-line robotics or have simply become costly anachronisms.

Among the more striking designs on the 212 Inter was the first collaboration between Ferrari and Pinin Farina, a cabriolet on chassis 0117 E delivered June 17, 1952. It was a low-line two-seater distinguished by a grille of generous dimensions, a hood with double air intakes, and a sweeping integrated fenderline that combined a subtle but distinctive return of the taillight pod into the rear fender.

In the early 1950s, the distinction between road car and race car was still of little consequence, and several of Ferrari's most alluring *competizione* also made superb berlinetta and spyder versions for the road. Of the latter, the short-lived Type 225 S stands out as one of Maranello's most intriguing dual-purpose models. How then did one distinguish between a Ferrari race car and a Ferrari sports car? If Tazio Nuvolari was driving, it was a race car.

With sports cars continually profiting from the lessons of the race track, the outcome was often an interim model like the 225 S. While the Barchetta would become the most popular Ferrari body style on the Types 166, 195 S, and 212 chassis, the 225 S was by far the most exciting open car of the early 1950s. A listing of serial numbers shows that about 20 were built during the car's single year of production, 1952, and that all but one had coachwork by Vignale—twelve spyders and seven berlinettas. Of those, around half-a-dozen had the Tuboscocca form of chassis/frame with double outer tubes, one above the other joined by a truss-like arrangement, with additional tubing used to create a skeleton outline of the body shape to which hand-formed panels could be mounted.

With its top lowered, the Pinin Farina cabriolet shows off its sleek, sporty styling lines, a fast fender sweep to the rear, accented only by the wheel arches, and a subtle but distinctive return of the taillight pod into the rear fender. The slight curve into the rear fender was the only line breaking up the car's profile.

The 225 Sport followed the design of the 212 Inter, with a Colombo short-block V-12 bored and stroked to 70x58.8 mm and a cubic capacity of 2.7 liters.

Essentially an engine variation, the 225 S shared the 212's chassis, with double wishbone, transleaf spring front, and rigid axle semi-elliptic spring rear suspension, with the same physical dimensions: a wheelbase of 88.7 inches with front and rear tracks of 50.4 inches and 49.25 inches, respectively. The only notable difference was that the 225 S used 5.25x16 tires at the front compared to the 212 Inter's 5.50x16. Rear tires were identical at 6.50x16. It was the car's styling, more than anything else, that set it apart from other Ferraris of the period.

In May 1952, the car originally driven for Ferrari by Piero Taruffi was sold through a dealer in Rome to Roberto Bonami, who campaigned the 225 Sport throughout South America, winning the 1953 Buenos Aires 1,000-km race and the Argentine Sports Car Championship in both 1952 and 1953. Two years later, on January 23, 1955, this same car finished sixth over-all in the 1,000 km of Buenos Aires. It has led what most would call a charmed life—never crashed, never abused, still with its original engine, and in good hands from the day it was built.

It's unlikely that Taruffi's car will ever again visit the abusive pavement of a road course, but like all great things past, this composite of steel and alloy has become greater than the sum of its parts. An icon. Something Enzo Ferrari probably hadn't envisioned in 1947, when his cars were merely "small, red and ugly."

Chapter Two

Carrozzeria
Ferrari and the Italian Ateliers

By the mid-1950s, Ferrari was producing a substantial number of road cars, and the separation between these cars and those built for competition was becoming more clearly defined. However, to say that there were production Ferraris was still a bit of a stretch. The design and construction of bodies remained the work of the individual carrozzeria, although Ferrari had by now settled on Pinin Farina and Vignale as his two most-often called-upon coachbuilders.

The rarest and most desirable Ferrari road car ever produced was the 250 GTO. Introduced in 1962, this became the quintessential road/race car of the era. The bodies were produced for Ferrari by Scaglietti, and a total of 39 were built in 1962, 1963, and 1964. Essentially a refined 250 GT SWB Berlinetta, the cars were equipped with a modified 250 GT engine, six twin-throat Weber 38DCN carburetors, a five-speed all-synchromesh gearbox replacing the old four-speed, and a potent 300-horsepower output at 8,400 rpm. Noted Hans Tanner, ". . . the car was for all intents and purposes, a Testa Rossa with a roof." In order to be homologated, Ferrari was supposed to produce 100 examples; however, when pressed by the FIA, Il Commendatore said that the market for the car was already saturated and there were only a few men in the world who could master its ferocity! The FIA still granted Ferrari homologation for the 1963 and 1964 seasons. *Automobile Quarterly*

Vignale catered to a number of prominent postwar Italian auto makers. The carrozzeria was not that old, at least compared to many of its competitors such as Touring and Pinin Farina.

The Vignale brothers had established a small workshop in Turin's Grugliasco district in 1939; but it was not until after the war that Vignale became successful.

Vignale had moved to Turin, taken in a partner, Angelo Balma, and a young designer named Giovanni Michelotti. Within two years, Carrozzeria Vignale had become a recognized car body designer, and through the firm's work for Ferrari in the early 1950s, rose to international fame. From 1950 to 1953, the Vignale works produced bodies for Ferraris that won three Mille Miglia and one Carrera Panamericana.

During the early part of the 1950s, Ferrari road cars varied from the 212 series (which remained in production until October 1953) through the 340 America (1951-1952), 342 America (1952-1953), and the 375 America, introduced in 1953. These were the first road cars to successfully carry the Ferrari name beyond Italy, particularly in the United States, where Luigi Chinetti was establishing Ferrari as the most prestigious line of sports and racing cars in the country.

23

The Cisitalia, designed in 1947 by Battista Farina became the basis for virtually every sports car design of the late 1940s and early 1950s. The earliest Ferrari road cars resembled this design, as did the first Ferrari cabriolet. The Cisitalia introduced the ovoid grille, fender port holes, and fastback styling that would become familiar on Italian sports cars like the Ferrari 166 and 212.

Chinetti had some pretty tough competition in the early 1950s. Sharing the New York spotlight was automotive importer Max Hoffman, with his plush Frank Lloyd Wright-designed showroom in the heart of New York City and a line of stunning new sports cars from Porsche, BMW, and Mercedes-Benz. Like Chinetti, Hoffman had the pulse of America's sports car elite, and the battle for sales was fought all the way from the showroom floor to the pits of Watkins Glen.

At the same time Ferrari was building the 212 Inter and Export, he decided to add a larger car that would appeal more to the American market and serve as the basis for a new competition car capable of taking on the Cadillac- and Chrysler-engined Allards, which were now showing their tails to the smaller-engined Ferraris. The old adage that there is no substitute for cubic inches was proving itself true once again.

By the mid-1950s Ferrari would introduce the 410 Superamerica as a response to Detroit's high-

Carrozzeria Touring's design for the legendary 166 MM was not only revolutionary in form, utilizing the firm's exclusive "Superleggera" or "super-light" construction method of small, lightweight steel tubes to which the body panels were attached, but in its color scheme as well, sheathed in a unique blend of slightly metallicized red. Most of the 166 MMs were painted this color, which has become a Ferrari tradition. The 166 MM chassis were also fitted with a variety of coachbuilt designs by Italy's leading houses, including a coupe by Allemano, an early berlinetta bodied by Stabilimenti Farina, and sport berlinettas produced by both Vignale and Touring Superleggera. *Automobile Quarterly*

The short-lived 340 America and 342 America were replaced in 1953 by the improved 375 America. The 375 was truly directed at the American market and Luigi Chinetti's New York City clientele. Many of the models, such as this Vignale Cabriolet, were designed for touring, rather than competition. Vignale bodied only two or three chassis in the 375 series. Chassis 0353 AL was fitted with an "American" windshield typical of the period *Automobile Quarterly*

power V-8s. The road from 212 to Superamerica, however, was paved with interim models, a handful of rare and exceptional cars built in limited numbers from 1952 to 1956.

Among the early high-performance coachbuilt cars was the 340 America, a model that proved moderately successful; although of the 22 constructed, only 8 were road cars. It was followed in the winter of 1952–53 by the more luxurious 342 America. Like its predecessor, the 342 offered left-hand drive. (It was during the production of late 212 models that the first left-hand-drive Ferrari were built. Until then, road cars had shared the same right-hand-drive layout as competition models.)

The 342 series was short-lived, concluding after only six examples—a stopgap between the 340 America and the new 375 America. The 375 had its engine capacity increased to 4.5 liters (275.8 ci) with a bore and stroke of 84x68 mm (3.307x2.68 inches) and three twin-choke Type 42DCZ Webers replacing the 40DCF used on the 342 America.

It had been designed principally for Chinetti's North American clientele, whereas the companion 250 Europa, also introduced in 1953, was intended for the European market. Both models made their debut at the Paris Auto Salon in October and, except for engines, were almost identical. The Europa had a 3-liter V-12. Production of the 375 America ended in

Among the more eclectic designs on the 410 Superamerica was a Ghia show car inspired by the carrozzeria's collaboration with American designer Virgil Exner and Chrysler. Ghia produced an entire series of concept cars for Exner, and stylist Mario Savonuzzi resumed the theme originally created for Exner's Gilda and Chrysler Dart concept cars with the 410 Superamerica. This was the most "Americanized" Ferrari ever produced.

1954 after approximately 13 cars were built, the majority of which were bodied as coupes by Pinin Farina.

For Americans, the construction of coachbuilt cars was a thing of the past, as outdated in the 1950s as a Duesenberg. In Europe, the advent of unitbody construction was also diminishing the demand and capability for producing bespoke coachwork. Ferrari, however, was an exception, still building cars in the manner of a decade before, delivering rolling chassis to local carrozzeria. Early on, Ferrari had relied on Touring and Stabilimenti Farina for designs. The latter, which opened its doors in 1905, was one of the oldest body builders in Turin. From Farina came such talented designers as Mario Boano, Giovanni Michelotti, and of

course, Battista Farina, who established his own carrozzeria in 1930. Beginning in 1950, Pinin Farina took the place of Stabilimenti Farina, which closed its doors. Battista Farina and his son, Sergio, began working closely with Maranello to design coachwork equal to the expectations of Ferrari owners.

The 410 Superamerica was a road car in the fullest sense, as its size and weight, an average of 3,500 lb, would have given it a decided handicap in racing. The handling and ride characteristics of the 410 Superamerica were better suited to vast open highways and cross-country touring than to winding mountain roads and city traffic. Given a good stretch of blacktop, the 4.9-liter V-12 could propel the 410 well into triple digits.

The Superamerica's interior was more finely detailed than any previous Ferrari model. The car used a four-speed synchronized (Porsche-type) transmission but with different gear ratios than the 375 America. The most disconcerting feature of the transmission was that on the majority of cars, first gear was found forward and to the right, and fourth was back and to the left.

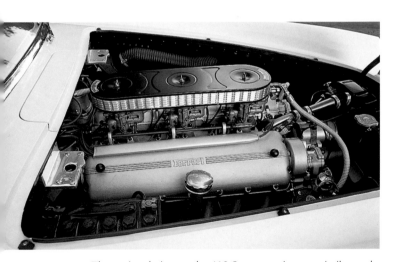

The engine design on the 410 Superamerica was similar to the ones employed on the 1951 F1 and on all sports cars until 1954. Displacement, however, was brought to the 5.0-liter limit through the use of new liners. The Lampredi-designed, long-block, 60-degree V-12 displaced 4,962 cc with a 88x68-mm bore and stroke, 8.5:1 compression ratio, and output of 340 hp at 6,000 rpm.

Recalls Sergio Pininfarina, (the coachbuilder had formally changed the spelling of its name in 1958, after the design firm opened new facilities in Grugliasco, outside of Turin). "After the war, in 1947, my father designed the best car he ever did, the Cisitalia. I think it set the pace for the design of sports cars throughout the next decade."

Indeed, it is virtually impossible to look at any European sports car designed in the 1950s and not see some resemblance to the Cisitalia. "As I look at it today it is still so simple, so well proportioned, a masterpiece, difficult to add anything to. . . ." said Pininfarina.

The 1950s were an important period for the Pinin Farina factory as it began to work with Ferrari. "In Italy, I would say we began to work with all the automobile manufacturers, and in Europe, with Peugeot, in England British Leyland, and some Japanese firms. My father was also the first Italian to design an American-built car, the Nash Ambassador," adds Pininfarina with a note of pride. But it was Enzo Ferrari who brought the most prominence to Pinin Farina—not for the volume of work Maranello provided, but rather for the adulation each new design received. Pinin Farina has since designed almost every Ferrari road car produced in the last 45 years!

Explains Sergio Pininfarina, "My inclination for sports cars is understood when you realize that when I was 25 years old, in 1951, my father gave me responsibility of the Ferrari section. Can you imagine a young engineer being responsible for the relation with Mr. Ferrari? He was a difficult man, a great man, a man that, with my father, gave me my point of reference for the love and dedication to automobiles."

The car's elegant profile was accentuated by a wraparound backlight, slightly finned rear fenders, and a distinctive rear fender cleave that swept downward to the rockers, creating a sweep panel effect from the doors forward. The Pinin Farina design for the 410 Superamerica also incorporated side vents located just aft of the front wheel openings. They had been common on competition cars and had been seen on the one-off Farina 250 GT Berlinetta at Paris, but this marked the first application on a Ferrari road car. They would become a trademark of the Superamerica and subsequently appear on nearly all Ferraris.

The production 250 MM carried on the Ferrari practice of independent front suspension with unequal length A-arms and transverse leaf spring. The rear setup was still a live axle, two semi-elliptic springs, and twin parallel trailing arms on each side which took braking and acceleration torque in addition to positioning the axle. The wheelbase, measuring 94.5 inches, was the shortest Ferrari had built since the 212 Export at 88.6 inches and the 166 MM at 86.6 inches. The front and rear track were identical to the 225 Export and 225 MM at 51.5 inches and 52.0 inches, respectively.

The cockpit of the 250 MM was just that, a place for the *pilota*, a traditional right-hand-drive racing configuration with two large combination gauges, bucket-type seats, and a large, wood-rimmed steering wheel. The 250 MM was equipped with a new four-speed all-synchromesh transmission.

Although Pinin Farina had created several significant cars for Ferrari by 1956, the design of the 410 Superamerica was perhaps the most important in cementing the bond between these two great companies. The 410 Superamerica was one of the most dynamic road car designs of the decade. Throughout Ferrari's first half century, few cars have been as influential in the world of automotive design.

The debut of Maranello's latest road car turned more than a few heads. The styling of the Superamerica would become the foundation for the 250 GT PF coupe, the original 250 GT Berlinetta "Tour de France" design, and would influence strongly the 250 GT Cabriolet and Spyder California with its distinctive rear fender kick-up.

Displacement for the 250 MM engine was 2,953cc (180ci) with a 73x58-mm bore and stroke (2.870x2.315 inches) and compression of 9.2:1. The Colombo-designed V-12 had 12 intake ports with the plugs on the outside of the heads. The air/fuel mix was delivered via three Weber 36 IFC/4 twin-choke, downdraft carburetors.

Above and Right
While each 250 MM varied in appearance, 0332 MM was highly distinguished by Vignale's use of faired-in headlights, a front-leaning stance, and foreshortened front fenders. Notable Vignale traits were the front wing, portholes, triangular vents in the rear fenders, and air ducts in the rocker panels.

Preceding the 410 Superamerica was a 375 concept car displayed at the Turin auto show in 1955. The styling of this sensational coupe, in white with contrasting black roof, clearly predicted the bodylines and color scheme of Pinin Farina's forthcoming 410 Superamerica show car. Renowned Ferrari historian Antoine Prunet, wrote that the 410 ". . . represented important progress in the design of the engine, the chassis, and the body."

As a bare chassis and engine displaying Ferrari's latest developments, the 410 Superamerica was shown at the Paris Salon in October 1955 and with

The 250 GT Berlinetta "Tour de France" was introduced for the 1956 racing season. Powered by a Colombo-based 60-degree V-12, developing 260 hp at 7,000 rpm, the Tour de France became Ferrari's customer competition model. All of the cars in this series had odd serial numbers, making them "production" road cars. They received FIA homologation because the mechanical specifications were identical to the Boano/Ellena coupes being built at the same time. Later "Tour de France" models (1958) had a redesigned front end more closely styled to the 250 GT Spyder California. *Automobile Quarterly*

the Pinin Farina body the following February. As a successor to the 375, the 410 used many of the same components along with the very successful Lampredi-designed V-12 engine that had won the 24 Heures du Mans, the Buenos Aires 1,000 km, and the Pan American road race.

The Lampredi V-12, increased to almost 5 liters, was given new cylinder barrels of an extreme 88-mm (3.46-inch) bore, while the 68-mm (2.68-inch) stroke was retained, giving the engine a displacement of 4,961.576cc (302.7ci). Using three twin-choke type 42DCZ Weber downdraft carburetors and a compression ratio of 8.5:1,

the 60-degree V-12 now delivered 340 hp at 6,000 rpm, and later versions, produced in 1958 and 1959 with 9:1 compression, developed a staggering 400 hp at 6,500 rpm. Of course, at this point in history, Ferrari was planning to sell cars in the United States where the horsepower wars raged and cars with such power were almost the *sine quahon*. However, for Ferrari, this was the largest displacement engine to yet power a touring car.

The chassis design of the 410 employed designs already in use on the 250 GT, specifically the front suspension, where the single transverse leaf spring used to

A factory-built steel-bodied car, this 250 GT SWB Berlinetta is reputed to have been a hill climb racer fitted with the Type 168 competition motor, ribbed gearbox, larger carburetors, higher compression pistons, the big fuel tank, external quick-fill gas cap, and quick-lift jacks. Something of a hybrid, it combines competition and lusso traits. However, this car is definitely set up for competition. Not unusual in the early 1950s, but less common in the 1960s.

support the A-arms on the 375 was replaced by coil springs, as had been done on the Europa GT. Both the front and rear track were also increased from the 375 by 130 mm to 58.4 inches and 58.2 inches, respectively. Chassis length remained at 110 inches until the 1958 and 1959 models, which were reduced to 102.3 inches.

Although no two 410 Superamericas were exactly alike, those bodied by Pinin Farina were similar in appearance and considered the most aggressive yet offered on a Ferrari road car.

In 1956, the 410 Superamerica was without peer, except for the Mercedes-Benz 300SL, and then only in terms of styling. In performance and price, the Ferrari was alone in its class. At the New York Auto Show, a 410 Superamerica of nearly identical design to the Belgian show car was offered by Chinetti at $16,800. The Mercedes-Benz 300SL from Max Hoffman was nearly $10,000 less.

With such a high price it is no wonder only 14 Superamericas were produced. Ghia and Boano also produced coachwork for this model: Ghia one coupe— the radical Chrysler Gilda and Dart-inspired 410 Superamerica, and Boano a convertible and a coupe. Pinin Farina also prepared a luxury custom-built

The interior of the production 250 GT SWB Berlinettas was plush for a competition-based design. This example has unusual dark green leather upholstery, an interesting contrast to the bright yellow exterior.

model, the Superfast I, No. 0483 SA. This was a very special coupe on a shortened 410 SA chassis which had been fitted with the twin-ignition racing engine used in the Scaglietti-bodied 410 Sport spyders. Other features of the Grugliasco designer's genius on this car were faired headlights, the large oval grille, and pillarless windscreen.

Well into the 1950s, the race car and road car were still relatively interchangeable. Early in 1952, Ferrari had decided to continue development of the short-block Colombo-designed V-12, even though the larger long-block Lampredi engine had been successfully converted from a 4.5-liter Grand Prix engine into a sports car powerplant.

Since its introduction, Ferrari had continually improved upon the original Colombo-designed V-12, increasing the displacement from an initial 1.5 liters to

2.7 liters. In the spring of 1952, another manipulation of the bore and stroke resulted in doubling the engine's original swept volume.

The new 250 Sport engine, while maintaining the stroke at 58.8 mm (2.32 inches), had the bore increased from 70 mm to 73 mm (2.875 inches), for a total displacement of 2,953cc (180ci). This new engine was fitted with pistons giving a robust 9.0:1 compression ratio, and when paired with three Weber 36 DCF carburetors was capable of producing 230 hp at 7,500 rpm.

The revised engine was mounted in a Vignale-bodied Berlinetta similar in appearance to the older 225 Sport, and this was the car Giovanni Bracco drove to victory in the 1952 Mille Miglia.

Ferrari historian Hans Tanner described the 1952 Italian road race as one of the greatest battles in the history of motor racing, as Bracco took on the whole of the Mercedes-Benz team. Up against bad weather and the incomparable Karl Kling driving a 300SL, Bracco battled for the lead, gaining and losing it several times until the final leg of the race over the Futa Pass. "Using his knowledge of the treacherous road," wrote Tanner, "Bracco caught up with and passed the Mercedes. When he reached Bologna at the foot of the pass, he was four minutes ahead of Kling, a lead he maintained for the balance of the race through Modena, Reggio, Emilia and Piacenza." This was the only defeat Mercedes-Benz suffered in the 1952 season.

Convinced by the success of the 250 Sport during a full season of racing, Ferrari decided to put this newly developed engine into a series-built chassis. However, time was short, and at the 1952 Paris Motor Show only a bare chassis and engine were displayed. Nevertheless, the 250 Sport's legendary season was enough to generate orders for a production version. The Paris Motor Show chassis was sold in the fall of that same year to Italian movie director Roberto Rossellini and given to Carrozzeria Vignale for completion as a competition spyder.

The production 250 MM was equipped with 12-port heads and three four-choke 36 IFC/4 Webers. Output was increased from the 250 Sport's 220 hp at 7,000 rpm to 240 hp at 7,200 rpm. The 250 MM was produced in both berlinetta and spyder configurations with the majority in berlinetta form bodied by Pinin

Farina. A total of 12 spyders were built by Vignale in two distinct series.

At the time, Ferrari had looked upon the 250 Sport merely as a normal evolution of a well-proven and time-tested design. But rather than the last throes of the old Colombo engine, the 250 Sport marked the beginning of Ferrari's longest-running series: the 250 GT. For nearly a decade, some 3,500 motors of almost identical design would power road car and race car alike.

Within Ferrari lineage, the 250 GT SWB Berlinetta was one of those rare cars afforded legendary status by sports car enthusiasts from the day of its introduction. It was simply the right car at the right moment, introduced on the heels of one great design—the 250 GT Berlinetta "Tour de France"—and preceding an even greater car—the Ferrari 250 GTO. The 250 GT SWB Berlinetta was the bridge between two of Ferrari's most significant road and race cars of the 1950s and 1960s.

The design for the 250 GT Berlinetta "Tour de France" followed the tragic Mercedes-Benz 300SLR accident at Le Mans in 1955, where driver Pierre Levegh and 80 spectators were killed after his failed attempt to avoid hitting a slower car. This horrible accident marked a turning point for sports car racing, which by 1955 had progressed to the point where competition sports cars were closer to Grand Prix cars than road cars. As a result, the Federation Internationale de l'Automobile (FIA) created new racing classes under the title Grand Touring. With help from Pinin Farina, Ferrari was ready to compete in the GT category with a brand new sports car, the 1956 250 GT Berlinetta.

A berlinetta ("little sedan" in Italian) was a lightweight, streamlined body trimmed for racing. Interiors were afforded minimal trim, insulation, and accessories, making them louder and less comfortable, but not unbearable. As each car was essentially built to order, some were more luxuriously appointed than others.

The "Tour de France," a name affectionately given the early 250 GTs following their domination of the 10-day race in 1956, remained in production until 1959, by which time the new SWB Berlinetta was waiting in the wings.

A quick change to colder plugs, racing tires, and the addition of a roll bar, and the 250 GT SWB Berlinetta could stand its ground against purpose-built racers in any sports car event from the Tourist Trophy at Goodwood to the 24 Hours of Le Mans.

Far removed from the competition scene was another Ferrari also called 250 GT, a pure road car produced by Pininfarina. The 250 GT PF coupe became the first standard-production Ferrari sports car. Thus, the Gran Turismo initials have been variously applied to a number of Ferraris. The 250 GT SWB Berlinetta, however, was by no means a production car.

Giotto Bizzarrini, Carlo Chiti, and Mauro Forghieri had completed development of the prototype in 1959, using a shortened 94.5-inch wheelbase. The new car used a solid rear axle, but it was located in such a way that an independent rear suspension would have provided no advantage. The front suspension used wishbones and coil springs with an antiroll bar.

The rigid rear axle used leaf springs and radius arms.

Bizzarini's goal had been to improve the handling of the long-wheelbase 250 GT, and this he accomplished with the SWB Berlinetta. Although the pure road cars (lussos) were more softly sprung, the hard suspension of the competition version gave the 250 SWB terrific cornering power.

Ferrari unveiled the 250 GT SWB Berlinetta at the Paris Auto Show in October 1959. On the short wheelbase, overall length was only 163.5 inches. The blunt-looking fastback carried a classic Colombo-designed 60-degree, 3-liter V-12 beneath its elongated hood.

As a result of the car's redesign, shorter overall length, reduced weight, and increased output—280 hp at 7,000 rpm versus 260 hp at 7,000 rpm for the "Tour de France"—the SWB 250 GT was faster and handled better than its predecessors, making it an even more daunting competitor. All of the cars were equipped with four-speed synchromesh gearboxes and later models were offered with electric overdrive. The 250 GT SWB Berlinetta was also the first GT Ferrari sold with disc brakes. The hit of the Paris salon, order books were soon full, much to the frustration of would-be owners who were given no delivery date if their names were not known to be directly related to racing!

The body, designed by Pininfarina, was produced for Ferrari by Scaglietti in Modena. In creating a design to fit the shortened wheelbase, Pininfarina used no quarter windows, adding to the car's aggressive and shortened appearance. Most of the bodies were steel, with aluminum doors, hood, and trunk lid, although a few all-aluminum SWB bodies were built to order for competition. Pininfarina manufactured certain components for the steel-bodied cars while the doors, hoods, and deck lids were constructed at Scaglietti.

Special racing versions of the 250 GT SWB, with either all-alloy, or steel-and-alloy bodies, could be equipped with a larger fuel tank, necessitating relocation of the spare tire directly under the rear window. Additionally, a few 250 GT SWB Competition were built with tuned, 300 hp Testa Rossa engines with six carburetors.

When introduced, the 250 GT SWB was a contemporary to the Aston Martin DB 2/4 MK III, the Jaguar XK-150 S, Maserati 3500, Mercedes-Benz 300SL, and the Chevrolet Corvette. As a road car, it was without peer, and in competition, the 250 GTs quickly ran up a string of victories throughout Europe. In 1960, SWB Berlinettas won the Tourist Trophy race, the Tour de France, and the 1,000 km of Paris at Montlhéry. And in 1961, Stirling Moss, driving Rob Walker's SWB, won the Tourist Trophy for Ferrari a second time. In fact, during 1961 so many class wins were collected by SWB Berlinettas that when the season came to a close, Ferrari owned the GT class in the Constructor's Championship.

With a top speed of around 150 mph, the 250 GT SWB Berlinetta was one of the fastest sports cars of its time, a driver's car with nimble handling and superb balance, that allowed it to be driven hard into corners as well as flat out on a straight-away. It was, as one driver wrote, "...so easy and comfortable to drive fast, and so sure footed." The 250 GT SWB, in either lusso or competition version, wrote Hans Tanner, "...more than any Ferrari before or since, was a car equally at home on a race track or a boulevard." There were fewer than 200 examples built from late 1959 until early 1963.

Throughout Ferrari's early history, the road from Maranello was paved with cars like the SWB Berlinetta. Road cars that could go racing, and race cars that could go touring.

According to factory notes, a few steel-bodied cars were built with the oversized competition fuel-filler cap in the left rear fender, a trait normally restricted to the light-weight cars where it was located in the upper left corner of the rear deck, as pictured.

Chapter Three

Grand Touring
The Elegant Ferrari

Word association. Ferrari? *Red*. Ferrari? *Fast*. Ferrari? *Luxury car*. Excuse me. *Luxury car?* That's how history has interpreted the 1964 Ferrari 500 Superfast and its predecessor, the 400 Superamerica, sports cars that were afforded an extra measure of interior luxury and comfort and thus distinguished from the more traditional race-bred road cars. The luxury gran turismo theme, however, is firmly rooted in the late-1950s, when Ferrari introduced the 410 Superamerica.

Aside from pure race cars, every Ferrari road car of the 1950s was luxurious for its time. There was, however, what many customers perceived to be a compromise in Ferrari's road-going coupes and berlinettas, which were tied more closely to the company's racing heritage than to the luxury and comfort one found in early postwar Alfa Romeo road cars, for example. This was a point Luigi Chinetti continually brought to Enzo Ferrari's attention, a bone of contention that seemed to have these men at odds throughout most of the 1960s.

The move to lusso styling, luxurious in an American context as Ferrari saw it, didn't come until the Pininfarina 250 GT 2+2 arrived in 1961. By the end of 1963 more than 950 had been delivered. For Ferrari these were phenomenal numbers.

Back in 1957, Ferrari had commenced series production of its first convertibles, the 250 GT Cabriolet. The first example, designed by Pininfarina, was shown at the 1957 Geneva auto show. The Cabriolets were not intended for competition, although with a 240-hp Colombo V-12 under the hood, there wasn't much aside from suspension, tuning, and a very plush interior that separated the car from its racing brethren. It was, perhaps, the ideal compromise between the two extremes.

The cabriolet's chassis was identical to that of the Boano coupes being produced at the same time using a welded oval tubular steel ladder-type frame with independent front and live rear axle and drum brakes.

A handsome if not stunning design, the early cars were noted for their dramatic grille, protruding Perspex-covered headlamps faired into the fenderlines, and bold vertical front bumperettes. The Pininfarina design featured a prominent air intake laid almost flat and extending nearly three-quarters of the hood's length.

Minor styling changes by Pininfarina to update the Spyder California included reshaping of the rear fenders to reduce their width, a new rear deck, and new one-piece taillights.

The Spyder California's dashboard configuration and finish was virtually identical to the earlier Pininfarina Cabriolet Series I cars. The Spyder California was not as luxuriously upholstered as the Cabriolets and had more purposeful interior trim. Some cars were delivered to special order with more luxurious interiors, while others were provided minimal trim for competition. The cars used a four-speed all-synchromesh transmission with direct drive in fourth.

This, along with the headlight and bumper design, gave the car an aggressive appearance from the front. The first series cars were limited to approximately two dozen examples, all of similar design, while later versions (another 12 cars produced in 1958-1959) featured a one-piece wraparound front bumper and less dramatic uncovered headlights pushed farther out to the corners, giving the front end more of a squared-off appearance. It is estimated that Series I production ran to around 40 examples, all with steel bodies by Pininfarina.

Despite the roadworthiness of the 250 GT Cabriolet, Luigi Chinetti was looking for a more aggressively styled GT convertible to sell. Chinetti's was not the only voice beckoning Ferrari to send Pininfarina back to the drawing board and his engineers to task on a revised chassis and suspension. Ferrari's West Coast distributor, John von Neumann, also agreed with Chinetti that the 250 GT Cabriolet was not the kind of Ferrari his customers wanted. Von Neumann felt that an open car with the characteristics of the lighter berlinettas would be very popular in the United States. Il Commendatore complied and gave approval for a special series to be built, the 250 GT Spyder California, which went into limited production in May 1958 and was built through 1960 on the long wheelbase GT Berlinetta chassis.

The revised coachwork, penned by Pininfarina, was manufactured at Modena in the workshops of Scaglietti. The cars were produced in two series, the long wheelbase, of which less than 50 were built, and the short wheelbase, a lighter weight, steel and aluminum-bodied version introduced in 1960 and built through 1963. Again, around 50 examples were built.

The 250 GT Spyder California SWB was equipped with the 60-degree V-12 rated at 280 horsepower at 7,000 rpm. As with the majority of 250 GTs, carburetion was by three Weber twin-choke downdraft carburetors.

The Pininfarina Cabriolet was a striking design built on the long wheelbase 102.3-inch 250 GT chassis. The body lines featured the pronounced rear fender kickup first shown on the prototype 410 Superamerica in 1956.

An even sportier version of the Spyder California, the short-wheelbase model, was built on the same chassis as the 250 GT SWB Berlinetta, measuring 7.9 inches less in wheelbase than the first series Spyder California. The SWB cars had essentially the same handling characteristics as the competition-bred berlinettas, and like the first series spyders, were genuine sports cars.

Among a handful that were pressed into competition was one entered by Luigi Chinetti's North American Racing Team (NART) and driven by Bob Grossman and Ferdinand Tavano to a fifth overall finish in the 1959 24 Hours of Le Mans. Several California Spyders were also fitted with competition engines, and upon special order supplied with all-aluminum bodies. The cars were normally made of steel with aluminum doors and deck lids.

The LWB Spyder California was produced in three series. About seven cars were built before the new LWB

250 GT Berlinetta engine and chassis were used. It is estimated that 27 second series cars were produced between the end of 1958 and the end of 1959. Most of the competition versions came out of this production run. The third series cars were fitted with the outside-plug V-12 engine, developed from the 250 Testa Rossa and equipped for the first time with disc brakes. Pininfarina's minor styling changes to update the cars included reshaping of the rear fenders to reduce their width, a new rear deck, and new one-piece taillights.

The SWB Spyder California made its debut at the Geneva Salon in March 1960. These examples were equipped with new heads and larger valves, increasing output by 20 hp to 280 hp at 7,000 rpm. (Competition engines were further increased to 300 hp with even larger valves, high-lift camshafts, and lighter-weight connecting rods and pistons.) The track was widened on SWB models, which were also the first to

switch from lever-type shock absorbers to adjustable telescopic units.

The Spyder California, in either wheelbase, was one of the first Ferrari "driver's cars," a car that was capable of exceptional speed and handling, yet comfortable and luxurious enough for daily driving. The last example (4167 GT) was sold in the United States in February 1963. Total production of the Spyder California in all versions was 47 long-wheelbase and 57 short-wheelbase models.

At the same time Scaglietti was turning out Spyder Californias, Ferrari took steps to further differentiate the Cabriolet model, introducing the Series II in 1959. This model was built concurrently with the Spyder California through 1962. Still on the long wheelbase, the Series II Cabriolet was even more of a boulevardier than the Series I with styling similar to the Pininfarina coupe, sans roof. It proved to be one of the most luxurious open Ferraris of the era.

Luxury via Maranello never looked better than it did in the next great Ferrari road car, the 250 GT Berlinetta Lusso, a breathtaking stretch of automobile

The 250 GT Cabriolet interior was plush for a Ferrari, with leather upholstered seating, console, door and kick panels, and a dashboard finished in a glare resistant matte black crinkle texture.

The engine in the 250 GT Cabriolet Series I was a Colombo-designed 60-degree V-12 with a bore and stroke of 73x58.8 mm (2.870x2.315 inches) displacing 2,953cc (180ci). The valve operation was by a single overhead camshaft on each bank with roller followers and rocker arms to inclined valves. With three twin-choke Weber carburetors and a compression ratio of 8.5:1, output was 240 hp at 7,000 rpm.

Chassis number 1803, this is the first 250 GT SWB Spyder California produced. Chassis specifications for the SWB were almost identical to those of the SWB Berlinetta. With a wheelbase of only 94.5 inches and lighter overall weight than the LWB Spyder California, the 1960–1963 models were the best handling of the series and the most attractively styled. The covered headlights of the early production cars were later abandoned, and the headlamp configuration changed slightly to accommodate chromed bezels. In general, this early design is considered better looking.

that even today rivals Ferrari's best efforts. Production of this model totaled only 350 from its introduction at the Paris Auto Show in October 1962 until the last body left Scaglietti in 1964.

The Lusso was the most daring new design from Pininfarina since the 410 Superamerica. With styling that resembled a touring version of the 250 GTO, the 250 GT Berlinetta Lusso is considered by many to be Pininfarina's greatest design for Ferrari.

With the Lusso, Sergio Pininfarina and his staff had delivered the first contemporary Ferrari road car of the 1960s. The Lusso body was a series of graceful curves, from the front fenders to the upturned rear spoiler, and free of any superfluous chrome trim to embellish its shape. Prunet described the new design as Pininfarina's escape from the "cubist" period, which had prevailed throughout most of the 250 GT and 410

SA models. The Lusso actually capitalized on many of those earlier designs. The forward-projected headlamps integrated in the fenders were straight off the Series I Pininfarina Cabriolet. Even the bumper design drew its shape from the bumperettes of the early cabriolet. Where the Lusso departed from past designs was in the rear fender treatment, which began at the windshield posts and carried all the way back through the tops of the doors until they met with the edge of the abbreviated deck lid—the only flat plane on the entire car. The design of the Lusso, noted Prunet, was all in accord with the aerodynamic theories of Dr. Professor Wunibald Kamm of the Stuttgart Techical University and proven by Pininfarina and Ferrari on the 250 GTO.

The Lusso's shape, which pioneered the aerodynamic vogue of the 1960s, was complemented by an interior that was the most luxurious in Ferrari history.

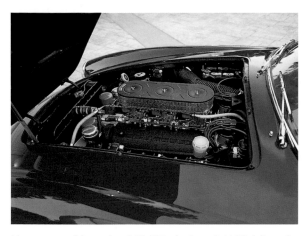

Not as powerful as other 250 GTs, the Lusso's V-12 delivered 250 hp at 7,000 rpm, some 30 hp less than the 250 GT SWB Berlinetta.

Within the roomy cabin, driver and passenger snugged into true bucket-type seats, upholstered in hand-sewn leather. The speedometer and tachometer were housed in two large pods in the center of the dashboard, with small secondary instruments behind the steering wheel. This feature was unique to the Lusso. There was also a full luggage shelf behind the seats, as well as a modest trunk, making this the first Ferrari road car that could carry enough luggage to actually take on the road.

Aside from exemplary styling and interior design, the 250 GT Berlinetta Lusso was also the fastest sports car of its day with a top speed of 150 mph at 7,400 rpm.

When the last Lusso pulled away from Maranello at the end of 1964, it marked the conclusion of the 250 GT era. Over a period of 10 years, the 250 GT designation was applied to nearly 2,500 Ferraris.

Although the engine and chassis of the 250 GT Berlinetta Lusso were pretty much standard Ferrari fare, the body design was Pininfarina's greatest design achievement of the 1960s. The Lusso was a genuine GT; as such, it was not well insulated, so engine noise (hardly a negative characteristic when it is a Ferrari V-12) filled the cockpit, making conversation difficult. Dean Batchelor noted that most of the noise was due to the low rear-axle gearing (high ratio), which caused the Lusso's V-12 to run at higher rpm.

The Lusso interior was unique to this model with a distinctive, if not unusual, placement of the primary gauges in the center of the dashboard. This, perhaps, gave the passenger an opportunity to note exactly how fast the car was going! For its time, the Lusso interior was plush with a great deal of attention paid to leather trim and carpeting. The dashboard was upholstered in a nonreflective black leather, lending both a luxurious and functional touch.

In profile, the Lusso displayed its stunning fenderlines flowing from the headlights through to the truncated rear deck lid. The Lusso's styling pioneered the aerodynamic vogue of the 1960s and inspired a number of subsequent designs, particularly the rear aspect which appeared again on the new 275 GTB. One interesting characteristic is the narrow width of the rear pillar, which gives the car a wraparound window effect and virtually no blind spot. During its two-year production run, approximately 350 Lussos were built.

The 330 GTC was an astounding combination of three Ferrari body styles, using elements from the 400 Superamerica, 500 Superfast, and 275 GTS. "A combination that could have been a disaster," as Ferrari historian Dean Batchelor once noted. Instead, the 330 GTC turned into one of Ferrari's most attractive two-place coupes. Although popular in Europe, sales of the 330 GTC were not exceptional in the United States. American buyers were looking for more aggressively styled and more powerful sports cars. Approximately 600 examples of the Ferrari 330 GTC were produced through the end of 1968.

While the Lusso had come closer to being a true touring car than any of its predecessors, Ferrari had already undertaken development of a genuine luxury model with the 400 Superamerica, which was built concurrently with the Lusso through 1964. The 400 Superamerica was also designed by Pininfarina, drawing on several auto show styling themes from the early 1960s, including the sensational Superfast II shown at the Turin motor show in 1960. The 400 Superamerica gave rise to the 500 Superamerica in 1964.

Essentially, Pininfarina had retained the aesthetic style of the aerodynamic coupes, but refined and tailored the lines of the 500 Superfast more closely to that of the 250 GT Berlinetta Lusso, which had been a styling triumph for Ferrari.

The 500 Superfast made its debut at the Geneva Motor Show in March 1964. It was a larger, more luxurious and more powerful replacement for the 400 Superamerica. Under the hood was a Colombo-based, 60-degree V-12, unique to the 500 Superfast. For this model, displacement was increased from the Superamerica's 3,967cc to 4,962cc (302.7ci). This was accomplished by using the 108-mm (4.26-inch) bore centers of the 1950 Lampredi-designed long-block 60-degree V-12 together with the general mechanical layout of the big Colombo V-12, thus creating a hybrid engine with an 88-mm (3.46-inch) bore and 68-mm (2.68-inch) stroke.

In 1964 the 500 Superfast had the most powerful engine available in a passenger car. The first series, about 25 examples, used the same four-speed, all-synchromesh transmission with electrically operated overdrive as the 400 Superamerica. The second series, an even dozen cars, built from late-1965 to the end of production in 1966, were little changed but did include new side louvers in the fenders and a new five-speed all-synchromesh gearbox, with direct drive in fourth gear.

The Superfast was built on a 104.2-inch wheelbase (50 mm longer than the 400 Superamerica LWB platform) with a 55.5-inch front and 55.2-inch rear track, both slightly wider than the 400. The suspension was of similar design: A-arms, coil springs, telescopic shock absorbers in front, and a live axle rear with semi-elliptic springs and telescopic shock absorbers. Other than the engine, mechanical specifi-

The 500 Superfast interior was the most luxurious of any Ferrari built up to that time with the use of wood veneers to accent the instrument panel and center console.

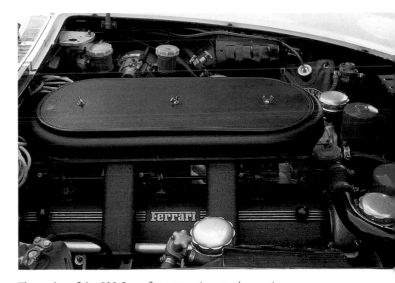

The engine of the 500 Superfast was unique to the car. It was effectively an extended Colombo engine with the same 108-mm spacing between the bore centers as the long-block Lampredi, but with removable heads. The 500 Superfast could attain a top speed of 174 mph.

Previous

With sleek, aerodynamic styling, the 500 Superfast was truly worthy of its name—which was originally coined by Pininfarina for a show car. The body design was based in part on the 250 GT Berlinetta Lusso and the Superfast's predecessor, the 400 Superamerica. Pininfarina relied heavily upon established Ferrari styling cues when designing new models. The Superfast, for example, had fender louvers similar to the 400 Superamerica's, which were derived from the earlier 410 Superamerica. Says designer Sergio Pininfarina, "Creating a new design is not always an easy task. On one hand, if you are following too much of a traditional look, you risk repeating yourself and not being innovative enough. On the other hand, I think it is right that I resist the temptation to make every car I design extraordinary."

cations for the 500 Superfast were almost identical to the companion 330 GT introduced in 1964.

The 500 Superfast was the most luxurious car Ferrari had built up to that time. The ultimate in front-engined Ferraris "for those who like the Rolls-Royce touch with their performance," as historian Hans Tanner wrote in 1974. But no one summed up the Super-

The 330 GTC used the same engine as the earlier 330 GT 2+2, a 300-hp Colombo-based V-12 displacing 3,967 cc (242 ci). The cars were equipped with a five-speed, all-synchromesh transmission built in-unit with the differential.

america better than Antoine Prunet who decreed that "Ferrari and Pininfarina had, without question, created quite well the Ferrari 'Royale.'"

Maranello's flagship coupe was luxuriously upholstered in buttery leather and accented with hand-rubbed wood trim on the instrument panel, dashboard, and center console. Power windows were a standard feature as was an AM/FM push-button radio.

Ferrari's advances in the field of luxury GTs reached an all-time high for the 1960s with the introduction of the 330 GTC and GTS models in 1966. Shown at Geneva in March, the 330 GTC was the ultimate Ferrari hybrid utilizing the chassis of the 275 GTB, the engine of the 330 GT 2+2 (introduced in 1964), and a body design by Pininfarina that combined the aerodynamic styling of the 400 Superamerica and 500 Superfast with the 275 GTS. As Dean Batchelor once noted, "a combination that could have been a disaster. . . ." However, in the skilled hands of Pininfarina, the juxtaposition of design elements from two berlinettas and a spyder turned into an extraordinarily attractive coupe.

A truly modern Ferrari for the times, it featured four-wheel fully independent suspension with unequal-length A-arms, coil springs, and telescopic shock absorbers, disc brakes on all four wheels, and a five-speed, all-synchromesh transmission built in-unit with the differential to deliver 300 hp from the Colombo-based V-12.

The 330 GTC was closer than any model had come to combining the power of a Ferrari V-12 with the unadulterated luxury of a touring car. It was fast, comfortable, and quiet. You could even have air conditioning.

Being all things to all people has always been a difficult task, but Ferrari made one remarkable overture to that end with the 330 GTC. Production lasted from mid-1966 to the end of 1968, at which time the engine was enlarged to 4.4 liters and the car was renamed the 365 GTC. This version was continued through 1969.

As Ferrari prepared to enter the 1970s, an entirely new line of road and competition cars was under development—cars that would once again break new ground in design, performance, and enineering.

A rear deck design traditional of Ferrari spyders such as the 330 GTS adapted surprising well to the coupe configuration of the 330 GTC, which actually preceded the 330 Spyder into production by six months.

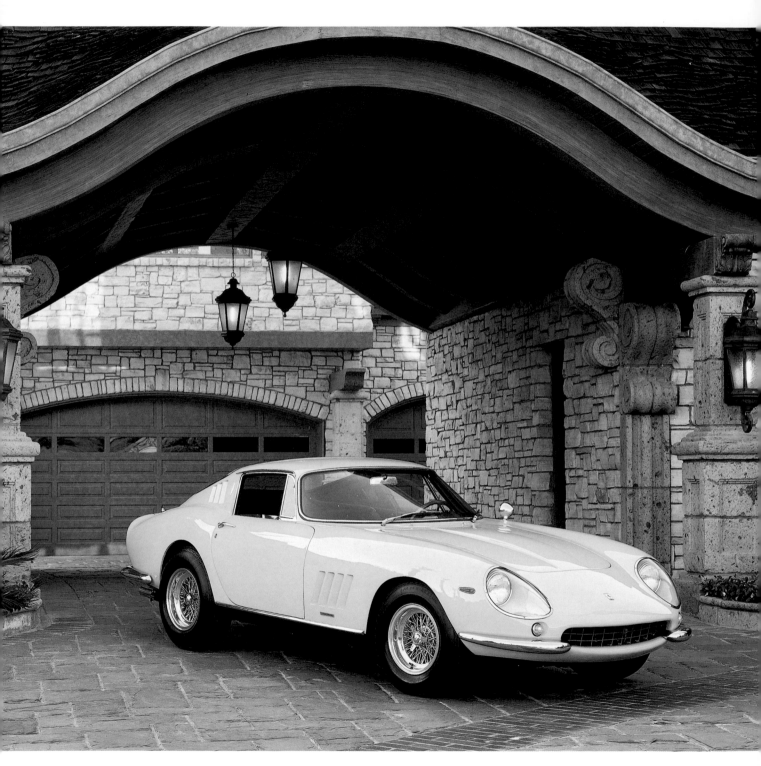

Chapter Four

Ferraris for All Seasons
The Great Road Cars

The most charismatic road car to come from Maranello after the 250 GT Berlinetta Lusso was the all-new 275 GTB. Originally introduced as a two-cam model in 1964, it was the first of Ferrari's now legendary 1960s-era Berlinettas offered to customers in touring or racing configurations.

Customers had the option of three Weber carburetors (with which the GTB was homologated for competition by the FIA) or a phalanx of six Weber 40 DCN/3s, endowing the engine with a brake horsepower capacity approaching 300. There was also a choice of construction offering a combination of steel and aluminum or all-alloy bodywork. Stylish Campagnolo 14-inch cast alloy wheels, recreating the design used on the 1963 Typo 156 Formula 1 cars, were standard, with the traditional Borrani wire wheels offered as an option.

Dean Batchelor noted in his *Illustrated Ferrari Buyer's Guide*, "The 275 series marked the progressive change in Ferrari design philosophy from thinly dis-

The car that led to the development of the 365 GTB/4, the Pininfarina-designed 275 GTB/4 Berlinetta. With the introduction of the Daytona, Ferrari bid farewell to the famous oval grille and fender-mounted headlight design that had been a hallmark since the late 1940s.

guised racers to comfortable and luxurious transportation vehicles. Because of the chassis changes—primarily the four-wheel independent suspension—the 275s were not only faster, but more comfortable than their predecessors."

Equipped with the Colombo-designed 60-degree V-12 displacing 3,286cc (77x58.8-mm bore and stroke) and dispensing 280 hp at 7,600 rpm with the triple Webers, the 275 GTB was the ultimate expression of Ferrari's ideology, a road car suitable for racing that gave up little, if anything, to purebred competition models. With that in mind, Ferrari also offered a limited number of 275 GTB/C models (about a dozen) stripped for out-and-out racing, equipped with a dry-sumped engine and lighter-weight sheet metal bodywork. Exactly two years after the introduction of the 275 GTB, the four-cam version made its world debut at the Paris Auto Show.

Ferrari was seldom first to introduce technical innovations. After all, Jaguar had been offering a double overhead cam (dohc) engine in its production and competition cars since the late 1940s. Over the same period, Ferrari had been content to offer a single overhead cam (sohc) engine (albeit a V-12) until the early 1960s. By that time, more and more European road

The 275 GTB/4 engine was another Colombo-based 60-degree V-12 design using double overhead camshafts on each bank. Compression ratio was 9.2:1 with fuel delivered by six Weber twin-choke downdraft carburetors. Output for the four-cam was rated at 300 hp at 8,000 rpm.

cars were appearing with four-cam engines beneath their hoods. Not only Jaguar, but Aston Martin, and in Italy, Alfa Romeo, Maserati, and a new Italian marque, Lamborghini. Enzo was more or less being enticed into the dohc market by his competition. If he was going to join in the fray, however, it would be on his terms.

The 275 GTB four-cam was derived from the 3.3- and 4-liter engines which had powered the 275 and 330 P2 prototypes of the 1965 racing season, engines which were themselves derivatives of Colombo designs dating as far back as 1957. Change, but not for the sake of change. It is interesting to note that between the first Ferrari 12-cylinder 125 model of 1947 and the 275 GTB of 1964, that is to say over a 17-year career, Ferrari's 60-degree V-12 engine had gained more than 140 percent in specific power! Never before had Ferrari offered such a competition-oriented road car to the public: double overhead cams, dry sump lubrication, six twin-throat Weber carburetors, and 300 hp at 8,000 rpm.

The new four-cam engine was introduced in a revised 275 GTB body at the October 1966 Paris Auto Show. The prototype GTB/4, with chassis number 8769 GT and engine 8769 GT, was designed by Pininfarina and built (as were nearly all 275 GT bodies) by Scaglietti.

Sergio Pininfarina's exotic styling for the 275 GTB and GTB/4 captured with great success the better elements of the competition-built 250 GTO, as well as, at the rear, the styling of the GTB Lusso. Pininfarina's approach was the perfect *leitmotif* for the new Berlinetta—a long, plunging hood, small oval radiator intake, streamlined covered headlights, pronounced hood bulge, truncated rear, and fastback roofline all perfectly harmonized to the contour of the steeply inclined and sharply curved windshield. The 275 GTB/4 was nothing short of aesthetic classicism, and if the car had any detractors, their only protest was that it too closely resembled the GTO. Hardly a fault.

The GTB/4 proved an incomparable dual-purpose sports car that could challenge the ability of even the most skilled drivers. Commented author Stanley Nowak, in his book, *Ferrari—Forty Years On the Road*, "Like all of the best Ferraris, driving [the GTB/4] automatically focused one's concentration on getting the most out of it. It responded in kind. The more one puts into it, the more one gets out of it. Like most Ferraris, it is intended for serious drivers." Says veteran race driver Phil Hill, "It was like a boulevard version of the GTO."

While there are enthusiasts who will argue the point, the majority will agree that the 275 GTB and GTB/4 were the best-looking berlinettas ever produced by Ferrari. Of the four-cam models, only about 280 examples were built. The rarest of all 275 GTB/4 models, however, were those *not* produced by Ferrari. At least, not directly.

Back in 1952, Luigi Chinetti had established Ferrari sales outlets in both Paris and New York City, where his showroom was located on the west side of Manhattan. His international racing exploits from Le Mans to the Carrera Panamericana had made him famous among sports car cognoscenti and granted him entrée into European and American café society. Luigi Chinetti was to Ferrari what Max Hoffman was

The styling of the 275 GTB and GTB/4 was an evolution of the 250 GTO and GT Berlinetta Lusso, the influences of which can be seen in this rear three-quarter view.

to Porsche—the conduit through which great cars would pass into the hands of racing and sports car enthusiasts of means.

When Chinetti decided to abandon the driver's seat in his late 50s, he had won at Montlhéry—Ferrari's first postwar victory in 1948—Le Mans in 1949, a second 12-Hours at Montlhéry with co-driver Jean Lucas, and the Carrera Panamericana with Piero Taruffi in 1951. He had also become a prominent figure in U.S. sports car racing, having placed cars in the hands of friends like Bill Spear and Jim Kimberly, who contributed to Ferrari's growing popularity in North America. However, it was Chinetti's involve-

ment in developing two of Ferrari's most celebrated models, the 250 GT Spyder California and the 275 GTS/4 NART Spyder, that made him legendary among Ferraristi.

In his memoirs, *My Terrible Joys*, Enzo Ferrari barely mentioned Chinetti's name, yet without him, it's unlikely Enzo Ferrari would have had much to write about. History will remember Chinetti, who succumbed to a heart ailment in 1994, shortly after celebrating his 93rd birthday, as the man who truly built the Ferrari legend.

As a dealer and importer, Chinetti understood the American market, perhaps better than Hoffman. To

Within the production run of 275 GTB and 275 GTB/4 models, there were short-nose and long-nose versions, a slightly larger rear window, and exposed trunk hinges. The car pictured is the actual 1966 prototype built by Pininfarina and displayed by Ferrari at the 1966 Paris Auto Show.

The 275 GTB had been the first Ferrari road car to offer four-wheel independent suspension. The GTB/4 would be the first equipped with a dohc engine. Not what you could call a significant change in the model, at least from appearances, but from behind the wheel, the GTB/4 had a character that clearly set it apart from its sohc predecessor. Although it looked nearly identical, except for a prominent hood bulge, the GTB/4 offered owners a 300-hp dohc V-12.

please his customers, Luigi would not only challenge Ferrari's decisions, but at times he would go out on his own and have special Ferrari models produced at his own expense.

By the mid-1950s, he had moved the Ferrari dealership from Manhattan to Greenwich, Connecticut, where he formed the North American Racing Team, better known as NART, in 1956. It was to be an independent arm of Scuderia Ferrari, that on occasion would also represent the factory when Ferrari decided not to enter events under his own name. Over the years, NART became one of the most illustrious acronyms in American motorsports and a virtual who's who of legendary race drivers. Among those who drove for or were discovered by Chinetti were Mario Andretti, Dan Gurney, Masten Gregory, Pedro and Ricardo Rodriguez, Paul O'Shea, Richie Ginther, Phil Hill, Stirling Moss, Bob Bondurant, Sam Posey, Jim Kimberly, Brian Redman, and Denise McCluggage.

The 275 GTB chassis, with a wheelbase of just 94.5 inches, was a proven design of ladder-type welded tubes with a four-wheel independent suspension consisting of unequal-length A-arms, coil springs, and telescopic shock absorbers.

Over the 26-year period between 1956 and 1982, NART campaigned in more than 200 races with more than 150 different drivers.

Because of their friendship, Il Commendatore had granted Chinetti the right to use the Cavallino emblem as part of the NART insignia. However, all the decisions regarding the team were Chinetti's, and he found himself at odds with Ferrari. They were two very stubborn men heading at times in the same direction, and at others, quite the opposite way. They were, as former race driver and author Denise McCluggage once put it, "indeed similar. Similar in the way that Yin and Yang are similar. You know, like hills and valleys; you can't have one without the other."

Recalls McCluggage, who knew both men very well, "Luigi was more like the director, the *auteur* always behind the scenes, while Ferrari was always grandiose, the grand figure."

Next
Several GTBs were modified for racing by their owners, but Ferrari also addressed competition with the 265 GTB/C or GTB Competition, which was offered in the spring of 1966. While the GTB/C retained the general appearance of the GTB—from the exterior, the only obvious difference between the two was larger wheels and slightly flared wheelwells—mechanically the differences were really quite radical. Ferrari produced 12 275 GTB Competition cars between May and August 1966.

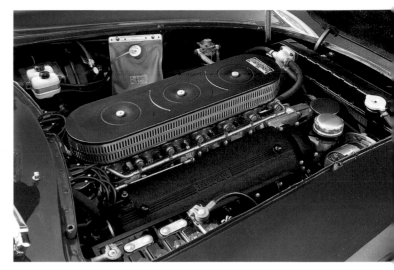

The 275 GTB/C engine had high-lift camshafts, 250 LM valves, reinforced pistons, a special crankshaft, and new Weber 40 DFI 3 carburetors. Built solely as a competition car, the GTB/C was equipped with a dry sump engine lubrication system with a separate oil reservoir.

The 275 GTB and GTB/C had two immense gauges—speedometer to the left and tachometer to the right—set into a wide oval instrument pod. Oil pressure and temperature gauges were positioned in between. The remaining instruments and switches were distributed across the center of the dashboard, practical in layout, yet accomplished with an elegant flair and just a hint of chrome embellishment.

The Other Ferrari Road Car: The 206GT Dino

The Dino is very much a part of the Ferrari road car legend, even though, technically, it is not a Ferrari, since the engines were built by Fiat.

In a very loose interpretation, the Dino was to Ferrari what the 914 was to Porsche, a less-expensive companion model. To Enzo Ferrari, however, the reasons for producing the Dino were very personal. The high-performance V-6

models were produced to commemorate Il Commendatore's son, Dino, who had died in 1956.

Dino Ferrari had suffered from muscular dystrophy since birth, but had much of his father's will. He managed to get through school and acquire a degree in engineering, but as his health began to fail, he was forced to spend most of his time in bed. Enzo and his close friend Vittorio Jano,

The Dino design by Pininfarina was one of the most curvaceous bodies ever produced for a sports car, a fact that contributed to the car's longevity. The cars bore no Ferrari emblems (the *cavallino* was added by a dealer), and the only reference was the Dino GT name next to the taillights and the Pininfarina body plate forward of the rear wheelwell. The cars were built on a 92.1-inch-wheelbase welded tubular-steel frame with four-wheel independent suspension and disc brakes. Only the 206GTs were bodied in aluminum.

one of Italy's greatest automotive engineers, would spend time with Dino in his room discussing the young Ferrari's ideas for a 1.5-liter racing engine. Dino had even written a two-part article on the design of a V-6 high-performance engine in the Italian magazine, *Velocita*.

Writing about Dino in his memoirs, Enzo Ferrari said that, "For reasons of mechanical efficiency [Dino] had finally come to the conclusion that the engine should be a V6 and we accepted his decision." Five months after Dino died, Ferrari created the 156 Dino engine.

Dino's inevitable death still came as a blow to Enzo. To honor his memory, Ferrari developed an entire line of Dino engines over a 10-year period for Formula 1, Formula 2, sports racing, and GT road cars.

Pininfarina bodied the first Dino road car to be powered by a rear-mounted V-6 eingine. The prototype known as the Dino 206GT Speciale was displayed at the Paris Motor Show in October 1965. A second version called the Dino Berlinetta GT was displayed at the 1966 Turin Motor Show, and like the earlier example, the engine was positioned longitudinally ahead of the rear axle. A third and final version made its debut at Turin in November 1967, this one with the Fiat-produced engine mounted transversely and built in-unit with a five-speed transaxle. An additional prototype was shown in Brussels the following year and early in 1969 production started at Scaglietti. By the end of the year roughly 150 Dinos had been built, all with aluminum bodies.

The 206GT was the first production Ferrari to be given only even chassis numbers (road cars had, with few exceptions, been serialized in odd number only) and the first not to wear either the Cavallino emblem or Ferrari name. It simply bore the signature "Dino GT" on the right corner of the body below the engine cover.

The majority of first series Dinos were sold in Italy and Europe, although a few were brought into the United States by Luigi Chinetti in 1969. The 206GT was replaced in 1969 by the 246GT, which remained in production through 1973. The 246GTS, featuring a removable targa-type roof panel, was added in 1972 and concluded Dino production in 1974.

The engine in the first Dino model, the 206GT, was a 180-hp, 65-degree V-6 displacing 1,987cc with a bore and stroke of 86x57 mm. The subsequent Dino engines used in the 246GT and GTS displaced 2,418cc with a 92.5x60-mm bore and stroke and increased output to 195 hp at 7,600 rpm.

The development of the NART Spyder in 1967 was the culmination to one of their most famous disagreements. To Luigi, spyders and convertibles were not interchangeable designs. Each had a well-defined purpose. When Chinetti had been a race driver, spyders were open competition models like the 166 MM, cars that had no windows or top, whereas a convertible had a folding top and wind-up windows. The fact that the differences were becoming less defined was the reason he had pressed Ferrari to build the 250 GT Spyder California in 1958 and then the SWB version in 1960.

By 1964, the Ferrari production car line had been divided into four models. First the lavish 500 Superfast, continuing the luxury image Ferrari had established in the early 1960s with the 410 and 400 Superamericas, then the sleek 330 GT 2+2, and the stunning 275 GTB and GTB/C Berlinettas. At the end of the line was the passionless 275 GTS, a spyder in name only,

The Type 226 V-12 used in the NART was based upon the P2 prototype racing engines that had been used by the factory team in 1965. The dual overhead camshafts were an obvious design change from the previous 3.3-liter GTB. The revised V-12 delivered up to 330 hp at 8,000 rpm and breathed through six Weber 40 DCN 17 carburetors, which are shown here.

built atop the GTB platform but with an entirely different body design. In appearance it was a much more conservative styling concept that retained none of the GTB's exquisite lines. To Chinetti, calling the 275 GTS a spyder was a sheer corruption of the word, and in terms of its spirit and intent, an unworthy replacement for the Spyder California.

Since Ferrari had little interest in building a new spyder for the American market, Chinetti's course was clear. His son, Luigi "Coco" Chinetti, Jr., had proposed to build a spyder based on the new 275 GTB/4 Berlinetta, arguably, the car Maranello should have produced instead of the ignoble 275 GTS. To accomplish this, they turned to Sergio Scaglietti, commissioning the carrozzeria to build a series of Competition Spyders exclusively for Chinetti Motors and NART. Scaglietti was an artist when it came to converting berlinettas into spyders, and what emerged from the Modena coachbuilder's palette was a hand-built masterpiece.

Chinetti had selected the greatest Ferrari of its time as the basis for the NART Spyder. Equipped with a four-cam V-12 breathing through six Weber 40 DCN 17 carburetors and delivering up to 330 hp at 8,000 rpm, the 275 GTB/4 was built atop a revised Type 596 all-independently suspended chassis, with the engine, prop-shaft tube and transaxle all rigidly mounted along the frame, as on the new Ferrari 330 GTC.

From the exterior, the four-cam model was easily distinguished from the standard 275 GTB by a raised central power bulge in the hood. It was also obvious whenever a driver applied substantial pressure to the throttle pedal—the GTB/4 could move from rest to 60 mph in 6.7 sec and reach a top speed in excess of 150 mph.

The rebodied berlinettas were delivered by Scaglietti to Chinetti Motors in Greenwich and sold in North America. Although Maranello scarcely acknowledged the existence of the 275 GTB/4 NART Spyder, it was to become one of Ferrari's most sought-after models.

The first car arrived stateside in February 1967. Stamped with chassis number 09437, it was painted Giallo Solare (sun yellow) and contrasted with a rich black leather interior. Enzo Ferrari did not believe that yellow was a proper color for a competition car bearing

Redesigning the stunning 275 GTB/4 Berlinetta into a Spyder was a task few would have undertaken, but Sergio Scaglietti took the Pininfarina fastback and cut the roof cleanly away leaving the same flowing rear fenderline intact and blending it perfectly into the rear deck lid.

his name. "Probably," said Chinetti in his Italian-accented English, "the scorers do not miss yellow so easily." Ferrari simply replied, "You have made a taxi cab." And so one more little battle of wills had been fought by these two giants; Ferrari, the car maker, and Chinetti, the image maker.

Following the 1967 Sebring race, Chinetti gave the car a complete overhaul and a new paint job—this time a deep burgundy—and sent it off to *Road & Track* magazine for testing. The article appearing in the September 1967 issue reported an impressive top speed of 155 mph, and it ran 99 mph during a 14.7-second standing-start 1/4-mile. *R&T* proclaimed it, "the most satisfying sports car in the world." After the road test, the car was delivered to the movie set of Steve McQueen's new film *The Thomas Crown Affair*. Although only briefly featured in the 1968 thriller, McQueen, an impassioned

The interior of the NART Spyder was straightforward in Ferrari tradition, no superfluous trim, just the necessary instruments and a hand-sewn leather dashboard. Seats were upholstered in black leather. The color scheme was a vivid contrast to the soft yellow exterior of the first car. Note the large metal-gated shifter used on the 275 series.

The first of their kind, the 1968 Ferrari 365 GTB/4 Berlinetta and 1969 Ferrari 365 GTS/4 Spyder prototypes. Both cars featured the Perspex nose band with concealed headlights, a stunning design that was not permitted in the United States. The prototype Daytona Spyder pictured (serial number 12851) was the only example built with the Perspex-covered European headlights. Any other Spyders with such covers were either retrofitted by the owner or the entire car converted from a European Berlinetta to a Spyder, a not too uncommon practice in the 1980s.

sports car enthusiast and accomplished race driver, was so taken with the NART Spyder that he purchased car 10453 from Chinetti.

Although nine examples hardly constitutes production, among Ferraris it is a respectable number, especially for a car that the factory had no intention of building. Thanks to Luigi Chinetti's vision of a proper spyder, today we have the 275 GTS/4, a car in which we can all delight until a time when such things as automobiles no longer matter and the world no longer resonates to the sounds of 12-cylinder engines.

The 275 GTB/4 Berlinetta and Spyder became the most recognized and desirable Ferrari models of their time, albeit, a very short time. Exactly two years after the four-cam prototype appeared on the Ferrari stand in Paris, the all-new 365 GTB/4 Daytona took its place.

"Berlinetta" and "spyder" are two of the most important words in the Ferrari language, words that define the essence of the automobile before one knows the year or model. So it was to be with the 365 GTB/4, which for many Ferrari collectors has become the ultimate example of the differing design strategies.

The Ferrari Daytona was first introduced in Europe as a Berlinetta in 1968 and then as a Spyder the following year. Displayed at the Paris Auto Salon, the prototype coupe was actually the third Daytona design created by Carrozzeria Pininfarina but the first to use the new 365 motor and to closely resemble the production car. Built on a 275 GTB chassis, every body panel and piece of glass was different from the later 365 GTB/4 production models, and the 1968 prototype was the only Daytona actually built by Pininfarina. The production cars were all produced for Ferrari by Scaglietti.

Since Ferrari first began offering road cars in the late 1940s, the Berlinetta design had evolved into one of Maranello's most popular body styles for both road and competition cars. Ferrari styling had for years dictated that every car have a dynamic grille, a pronounced, aggressive visage epitomized by such models as the 250 MM, 340 Mexico, and 250 GTO. For the Daytona, however, Sergio Pininfarina and his staff were about to take a detour, departing from all previous Ferrari models and abandoning for the first time the traditional oval grille that had become a Ferrari hallmark.

The Daytona's original design called for headlights concealed behind a clear plastic cover. The dynamic new design, however, was not in accordance with federal headlight height requirements, and the design had to be changed for export models. Ferrari found it necessary to design a second front end which positioned iodine headlamps in a retractable housing that mimicked the Perspex nose when the lights were off and "popped" up (Corvette style) when they were turned on. All models originally sold in the United States were so equipped.

Breaking from tradition was a difficult decision for Sergio Pininfarina. For more than a decade he had designed bodies for Ferrari that were imbued with a sense of heritage, and however different they may have been from model to model, there was always a distinctive look. The 250 GTO, 250 GTB Lusso, and 275 GTB had been the first cars to significantly advance aerodynamic design at Ferrari, but they still bore traditional Ferrari styling cues. Pininfarina was convinced that aerodynamics were now as important to the car's performance as the suspension and driveline.

Surrendering the aggressive oval grille design for the first time, the Daytona presented a sharp, thin line from the front, with the radiator intake forming a horizontal slit beneath the nose. In one bold stroke, Sergio Pininfarina had changed the Ferrari's formidable open mouth into a malevolent grin.

This new approach to front-end styling presented one unique challenge: where to place the headlights, which had for more than 20 years been a part of the fender design. With the 365 GTB/4, however, there were no front fenders, at least not in a classic sense. This brief

From fastback to flatback, the 365 GTB/4 Spyder's revised design featured a new deck lid and flush boot cover that blended perfectly into the body's curve. Compared with the Berlinetta, the Spyder was dramatically different. It appeared lower, even more virile than the coupe, and it was more fun to drive. Indeed, there was no substitute for the wind curling over the windshield and the aromas of the open road teasing around in the cockpit.

impasse led to the most dramatic styling change in Ferrari history—the elimination of faired-in headlamps.

For the 365 GTB/4, Pininfarina chose to set the headlamps back under clear rectangular covers, which blended with the line of the front deck. Small horizontal bumpers were set into either side of the radiator air intake, with small parking lights tucked in just above, and small, round marker lights positioned on each side of the front fenders. At least one prototype incorporating these changes was built in the late summer and early fall of 1968. On the final version, the paired headlamps were set slightly back from the nose of the car, but the entire nose was now covered by a single band of transparent plastic approximately eight inches high. This nose band wrapped around the front corners of the car to integrate parking and side marker light units, ending just short of the front wheel arches. Toward either end this plastic band was left essentially clear (there were fine white vertical lines on the inner surface) where it covered the four headlights. In the center, the inner surface of the perspex was painted black (still with fine white vertical lines), except for the very center which was left clear to display the rectangular Ferrari emblem attached to the bodywork underneath.

There was much more to the 365 GTB/4 than its radical new headlight design, however. The hood was a highly complex series of curves and one of the most difficult pieces on the entire car. On either side and approximately halfway back there were two recessed air vents, located in a low-pressure area and serving as outlets for warm air passing through the combined water and oil radiator. Adding to the complexity of the hood, the trailing edge was curved to conform to the base of the windshield, with the gap between the hood and windshield varying from a mere fraction of an inch at the sides to several inches along the centerline of the hood. At the same time the plane of the hood bent sharply upward along the rear edge, giving the effect of a louver and in theory directing the airflow up to the windshield rather than bluntly into it.

The large gap created by the curve of the hood as it rounded the windshield served a dual purpose as an additional outlet for engine compartment air and a storage space to park the windshield wipers. In theory the wipers were supposed to be removed from the line of vision through the windshield, thereby precluding annoying reflections on the windshield, and by tucking them behind the louver at the rear of the hood, improving aerodynamics. Actually, the wipers had to be parked in view in order to clean the windshield.

A factory press release noted that the large, double-curved windshield had "an extremely aerodynamic line" and was sharply angled to the rear. It was attached to the body without a visible rubber gasket, which was recessed to improve the smoothness of the lines and covered by a thin strip of bright metal surrounding the windshield.

There was a decidedly rakish angle to the Daytona's roofline, establishing a fastback appearance at the rear of the body before angling down to the deck lid. An extremely large and almost flat rear window was used on the Berlinetta. It was installed in a manner similar to that of the windshield and also surrounded by a thin strip of brightwork. The tail section of the fastback was taken up with the rear deck lid, which ended along the rear edge of the upper bodywork on the prototype but extended down between the paired round taillights on production versions.

With only a few exceptions—most notably the 1962 250 GT Lusso—Ferrari Berlinettas were notorious for restricted rear vision. The Daytona would not follow suit. In designing the 365 GTB/4, Pininfarina used taller side windows extending upward from the beltline to the flat roofline, allowing drivers improved over-the-shoulder visibility. The door glass featured front vent windows on each side and aft of the door glasses, in the rear sail panels, were rear-quarter windows, followed in turn by a set of crescent-shaped air outlet vents, which were painted black. The entire window ensemble was surrounded by bright thin metal frames and an additional piece of brightwork along the drip molding above the windows to accent the roofline. The large expanses of glass helped lighten the visual effect of the rear half of the car as well as provide good visibility for the driver.

In keeping with Pininfarina's decision to eliminate unnecessary embellishments, the trim around the windows was just about the only evidence of brightwork. Even conventional door handles were eliminated. Instead, small levers swiveled out parallel to the bottom of the door windows, almost looking like part of the window trim. On the rear center of each door there was a small key lock, and that was all Pininfarina allowed to impair the smooth flow of the body lines.

One of the most significant styling characteristics of the 365 GTB/4 was the "*trough-line*", a concave molding used to create a visual divide between the upper and lower body panels, without resorting to the use of chrome trim. Fully encircling three-fourths of the car, it extended the length of the body from behind the front wheel arches to those at the rear and then around the back of the body above the bumpers. The sides of the Daytona were also somewhat narrowed in appearance by the sharp inward slant of the rocker panels giving the car an almost barrel-sided roll between the wheel arches.

Filling the void left earlier in the year by the discontinued 275 GTB/4 Berlinetta, the all-new Daytona made an immediate splash when introduced at the Paris Salon. However, it was not immediately available, and Ferrari did not produce the cars in any great number until the last half of 1969. Although it was the first Ferrari to be built in quantity to meet the U.S. regulations, the European version was marketed first and the U.S.-legal cars were not available on a regular basis until mid-1970; real quantities did not arrive until early 1972, when the new U.S. Ferrari importers took over. In the eastern United States a partnership was formed by the Chinettis and Al Garthwaite. In the West, the importer was Modern Classic Motors in Reno, Nevada, owned by renowned car collector and casino owner Bill Harrah.

In all probability the 365 GTB/4 shown in Paris was the final Pininfarina prototype finished in a bright Ferrari racing red with a red-and-black interior. The prototype built on chassis 11795 stayed with the factory until it was sold to one of its Formula 1 drivers, Arturo Merzario, in December 1970. That car is currently in a private collection.

Interior of the Spyder was identical to that of the 365 GTB/4 Berlinetta.

Ironically, the car's most attractive feature, the Perspex-covered headlights, became its greatest handicap when Ferrari tried to sell the Daytonas stateside. The plastic-covered headlights were not in accordance with federal height requirements. Ferrari found it necessary to design a second front end for export which positioned iodine headlamps in a retractable housing that mimicked the Perspex nose when the lights were off and "popped" up (Corvette style) when they were turned on, at which point the entire aerodynamic theory of the Daytona's front end design went out the window. So much for artistic solutions!

The body of the new car was not the only innovation. In order to meet new Federal emissions regulations that took effect in the United States in 1968, Ferrari's engineers had to come up with an efficient, clean-burning engine. The 365 GTB/4 model designation followed the Ferrari custom of stating the displacement of a single cylinder, followed by a set of letters and numerals that further defined the car. Thus, the new berlinetta had 365cc per cylinder (precisely 4,390.35cc total displacement), was a Gran Turismo Berlinetta, and had an engine with four camshafts.

The new 60-degree, dohc V-12 was derived from earlier designs by Gioacchino Colombo and Aurelio Lampredi. Displacing 4.4 liters (268ci) and teamed with six Weber DCN20 twin-barrel 40-mm downdraft carburetors, the fed-legal Ferrari engine delivered 352 hp at 7,500 rpm, taking the drive through a ZF all-synchromesh five-speed transaxle built in-unit with the differential.

Following the 275 GTB/4, the Daytona had a four-wheel independent suspension comprised of unequal length A-arms with tubular shock absorbers, coil springs, and front and rear antiroll bars. The Daytonas were also equipped with Dunlop ventilated disc brakes on all four wheels.

Underneath, a welded tubular steel ladder frame supported the car's 94.5-inch wheelbase and wider-than-normal 56.6-inch front and rear track. The Berlinetta's broad stance was contrasted by an overall length of 174.2 inches.

At the time of its introduction in 1968, the 365 GTB/4 Berlinetta was the most expensive and fastest road car in Ferrari's 21-year history. Priced at just under $20,000, the Daytona was capable of reaching a top speed of 174 mph, according to the factory. *Road & Track* recorded 0 to 60 in 5.9 sec and a top speed of 173 mph, but who's quibbling?

Following the successful introduction of the Daytona Berlinetta, work began on a spyder version to be introduced in 1969. Although building spyders was something of a tradition with Ferrari, beheading the 365 GTB/4 flew in the face of reason.

Designed to take advantage of Europe's high-speed autoroutes, the Daytona was the most aerodynamic model in Ferrari's stable. Pininfarina claimed that the outline of the body had been developed, both in general lines and in many smaller details, in accordance with studies conducted in the wind tunnel at the Turin Polytechnic Institute. Aerodynamics was as much a part of the car's performance as the refined V-12 engine under the hood. If the roof was removed, the aerodynamic gains were gone with the wind! Making a Daytona Spyder was not logical. Of course, who said logic has anything to do with automobiles?

"In Europe, we are accustomed to thinking of a sports car as a berlinetta. On the contrary, a sports car for an American many times means a spyder," says Sergio Pininfarina.

In total, 1,383 Daytonas were produced, including 122 spyders, 96 of which were sold to customers in the United States.

Chapter Five

Contemporary Ferraris
Road Cars of the 1980s and 1990s

Racing has been the foundation for nearly all of Maranello's advancements in the design of road cars. One of the most significant was the development of the Boxer engine in 1964.

Ferrari's first flat, opposed (180-degree V-12) Boxer engine was a 12-cylinder, 1.5-liter Formula 1 engine with 11:1 compression ratio, Lucas fuel-injection, and output of 210 hp at 11,000 rpm.

The Boxer name was derived from the piston's reciprocating movement, back and forth, toward and away from each other, like two boxers sparring. The term, however, was actually of German origin, used to describe the layout of the early Porsche and Volkswagen four-cylinder engines, which were also of flat opposed design.

The 365 GT4 Berlinetta Boxer—Ferrari's first midengine production sports car (discounting the Dino) was fitted with a 4.4-liter production version of the competition engine in 1974. Mounted behind the driver and ahead of the rear axle, it delivered 380 hp at 7,200 rpm.

Pininfarina's penchant for displaying the Ferrari engine reached an all-time high with the F40. The transparent plastic engine cover gave everyone a clear look at the inner workings of this incredible sports car.

The 365 GT4 BB would be the first of an entire generation of new rear-engined 12-cylinder models that would remain in production for more than 20 years. The main body structure of the 365 GT4 was steel, with the hood, doors, and rear deck lid made of aluminum and the lower body panels constructed of fiberglass. As usual, the design was by Pininfarina with the actual body production handled by Scaglietti in Modena.

The cars used the latest Ferrari suspension technology, with unequal-length A-arms, coil springs, tubular shock absorbers, and antiroll bars front and rear.

In a review of the 365 GT4 BB, Dean Batchelor noted, "Handling is great for the enthusiast driver. The steering, which is heavy at low speeds, lightens up as speed increases and the tail heavy weight distribution (43/57 percent), which would normally cause oversteer, is offset by a suspension with understeer designed into it—resulting in an agile, maneuverable car."

The 365 GT4 BB was the first Ferrari road car in many years to actually give drivers a taste of what a race car felt like. Ferrari produced the car until late in 1976, when the 512 Berlinetta Boxer took its place. The body styling of the 512 was almost identical to that of its predecessor. Pininfarina's revised styling added a "chin spoiler," or air dam, beneath the egg-crate front grille

One of Ferrari's longest-lived road cars was a true boulevardier; the 400GT was introduced in 1976 and was succeeded by the 400i GT in 1979 and the 412 in 1985. These were the first full-size 2+2 luxury touring Ferraris to be equipped with automatic transmissions.

and air ducts on the lower body sides forward of the rear wheels. Other changes included the now-famous 512 BB taillight array, with two large round lenses per side, reprised on the 1995 Ferrari F 512 M.

The 512 BB employed the same blended media construction as the 365 GT4 BB, using steel for the main body structure; aluminum for the hood, doors, and engine cover; and glass fiber for the lower body panels. The use of glass fiber led to the most distinctive and memorable styling characteristic of both the 365 and 512: a solid division line between the upper and lower body panels. On the 365 the lower part was always painted matte black. The two-tone color scheme was also available as an option on the 512 BB.

Displacement of the Forghieri-based 180-degree V-12 engine used in the 512 BB was enlarged to 4,942 cc (up from 4,390 cc in the 365) by a bore increase of 1 mm to 87 mm, and an increase in the stroke of 7 mm to 78 mm. While output from the

revised Boxer engine was actually decreased by 5.2 percent (down from 380 hp to 360 hp), peak horsepower was reached at 6,200 revs instead of 7,200. An interesting trade-off.

Both the 365 and 512 Boxers were raced by private entrants, but their time in the sun was brief and the racing effort short-lived. It was by far, however, the best road car Ferrari had brought to market up to that time. Batchelor wrote of the 512 BB, "The Boxers are fantastic cars to drive, with little *raison d'être* other than the sheer pleasure of driving the ultimate sporting GT car." Almost 20 years after its introduction, the 512 BB with its razor-edged styling and incomparable midengine layout remains one of the most desirable of all Ferraris. A car that still looks like it's going 200 mph while standing still.

Evolution in design has led to many of Ferrari's most outstanding and best-loved road cars, but none became more ubiquitous than the 308 GTB and GTS,

For a car that was closer to a race car than a road car in performance and handling, the 512 BB provided driver and occupant with an exceptionally high level of interior comfort and trim.

the most recognized Ferrari model ever produced, thanks in part to the television series *Magnum P.I.*, starring Tom Selleck. But moreover, Ferrari enthusiasts found this the most practical driver in Ferrari's history.

Pininfarina stylists combined the best attributes of the 246 Dino and 365 GT Berlinetta Boxer in the 308's design. Suspension was all independent in the then-traditional Ferrari layout, and the cars were powered by a four-cam, 90-degree V-8 engine mounted transversely just ahead of the rear axle. The 308 offered a spirited 255 hp at 7,700 rpm, and drove through a five-speed transmission. An open version of the 308, with a removable roof section similar to that used on

Beneath Pininfarina's sculpted deck lid was an equally attractive engine. The Forghieri-based, opposed flat-12 was designed to look as impressive as it felt under full throttle.

the 246 Dino and Porsche 911 Targa, was added to the line in 1977.

The longest-running model in Ferrari history, the 308, continued on into the 1980s in improved versions, the 308GTBi, 308GTB Qv (quattrovalve), and 328 Berlinetta and Spyder.

Back in 1987, when Ferrari celebrated its fortieth anniversary, Modena introduced the F40. The name was chosen to commemorate the production of Ferrari automobiles from 1947 to 1987, but the F40 was no badge-engineered commemorative issue. It was the first Ferrari since the 512 BB that was closer to a race car than a road car. It was also the least-practical Ferrari ever produced. Although, in the spirit of the original sports cars built in Modena 40 years earlier, the F40 was the ideal model to honor Ferrari's anniversary year. A sports car pure and simple.

The body was a Kevlar, carbon-composite shell surrounding a tubular steel Kevlar and carbon-composite framework, to which Ferrari had fitted a 478-hp, twin turbocharged dohc four-valve V-8 engine and a highly articulated four-wheel independent suspension. Little more was needed to take an F40 into competition than some additional safety equipment and numbers on the doors.

A recessed latch released the light-weight doors, allowing the driver to climb or drop, depending upon one's style or build, into the contoured racing seat. Getting into or out of the F40 became a learned art. Until one mastered ingress and egress, bruised hips and shoulders were constant companions.

For the $250,000 originally asked by the factory (prices approached $1 million as speculators bought and resold cars throughout the late 1980s), buyers received a great deal of sensory gratification with the F40, but little else. The interior had a full complement of gauges, everything the driver needed to know, and nothing more. No 12-way power-adjustable seats with driver memory. No power windows or accessories.

The styling of the 512 Berlinetta Boxer was taken directly from the 365 GT4 BB and updated by designer Sergio Pininfarina with the addition of an under-grille spoiler, which squared up the front end, and NACA ducts on the lower body sides forward of the wheel openings.

Virtually no interior trim, not even door panels or door handles, you just pulled the cable slung in the hollow of the door and it unlatched. And no radio. Had there been one, it would have required a 300-watt system to boost the volume over the engine because the F40 had virtually no interior soundproofing. Even if it had, who needed music? The deep bass exhaust note under throttle, the treble whine of the V-8, and the rhythm of the Pirelli P Zeros beneath you were a symphony for the senses.

The F40 was pretty simple. You stepped on the gas pedal, the car went fast, very fast; you hit the brakes, it stopped; turned the wheel and it went where you pointed. Just the way Enzo Ferrari intended things to be.

The career of the flat 12 hadn't ended with the 512 BB (1976 to 1981) and 512 BBi (1981-1984). The design was continued in the next generation of Ferrari road cars, which began in 1985 with the all-new Testarossa.

In the fall of 1984, Ferrari unveiled the Testarossa in Modena on the site of the original Scuderia Ferrari facility in the heart of town. The name Testarossa, which means redhead, was taken from one of Ferrari's most legendary race cars, the 250 Testa Rossa, which had rampaged across Europe in the late 1950s. And like its namesake, the 1985 Testarossa was a radical departure from conventional Ferrari designs. Pininfarina had pulled out all the stops, taking form and function to a new level by essentially designing the body around the engine, a 4,942-cc flat 12 delivering

The 40th anniversary Ferrari, the F40, became one of the most speculative models in Ferrari history. At a suggested retail price of $250,000, the limited-edition cars soared to nearly $1 million as speculators and investors traded them like commodities until the sports car market crashed. Says Ferrari S.p.A Chairman and CEO Luca Cordero Di Montezemolo, "I am personally very happy that the market went back to a normal limit like it was in the early '80s because the last years, in my opinion, were mad years and this is not good."

The 348 was the first two-seat convertible since the 365 GTB/4 Daytona Spyder, last sold in 1974, and also the first midengine two-seat Ferrari Spider ever. (Ferrari changed the spelling of Spyder with a "y" when referring to the Daytona, to an "i" when addressing later models.) The Spider was the evolution of the 348 tb/ts series announced in 1989. Power for the midengine 348 convertible was Ferrari's proven 90-degree light-alloy V-8. Displacing 3,405cc with an 85x75-mm bore and stroke, output from the four-valve per cylinder motor was rated at 312 hp at 7,200 rpm, and 228.6 ft-lb of torque at 4,000 rpm. The transmission is a transverse five-speed gearbox.

390 hp at 6,300 rpm in European trim and 380 hp in U.S. specification.

The most outstanding aspect of the design was the horizontal air intake strakes rending their way through the doors and into the rear fenders. This became the car's most distinctive characteristic and one that has never been successfully duplicated, except by Ferrari in the Testarossa's two succeeding models, the 512 TR and F 512 M.

The F 512 M was a glorious revival of the 1991 512 TR, itself a generation beyond the Ferrari Testarossa. The F 512 M also drew upon history for its name, resurrected from the 512 Berlinetta Boxer. This car also had another historical imperative. It was to be the first interim Ferrari model in decades.

An improved version of the Testarossa, restyled by Pininfarina hard on the heels of the new F 355 Berlinetta and the 456 GT 2+2, the 1995 F 512 M was destined to be discontinued, and everyone knew it. This was a car that would be judged as few had. Not by the press, whose opinions are often taken too seriously, but by the very owners who would plunk down hard-earned lire for a car whose fate had already been sealed. The F 512 M was to be the end of the line for the Boxer engine. A line that concluded an 11-year run in 1996, when the F 512 M was officially replaced by the 1997 550 Maranello, the first front-engine Berlinetta since the 365 GTB/4 Daytona.

Without overdoing the technical analysis, one could say little of the original TR remained. Mechanically, the F 512 M was a generation beyond. The Formula 1-inspired Boxer design delivered a heart-pounding 440 hp at 6,750 rpm, a full 50 hp better than the old Testarossa and 12 more than the 512TR.

With 367 ft-lb of torque at 5,500 rpm, the new F 512 M had no difficulty vanquishing either of its predecessors. Zero-to-60 was a scant 4.6 sec, and top speed just 4 mph short of 200.

From the exterior, the most striking visual change in the Pininfarina styling was the aggressive front, reminiscent of the F40 and tempered with a touch of the new 456 GT's graceful form in and around the grille.

The F 512 M was a lighter, more powerful, more agile, and better-built version of the Testarossa, still as impressive in appearance as the original, generously wide on the exterior and incomprehensibly narrow inside, a Coke bottle mounted on aluminum caps and propelled by a rocket-like V-12 that could snatch your breath away at full song and leave you wishing for legendary roads to challenge. Indeed, the F 512 M was an interesting way to bid farewell to both the Testarossa and the venerable Boxer engine.

Traditionally, Ferrari's new model introductions were held in Italy and throughout Europe before the cars were shown in the United States. No automobile, let alone a Ferrari, has ever been introduced to the world on a city street. Of course, Ferrari is no ordinary automobile and Rodeo Drive in Beverly Hills, California, no ordinary street.

On Saturday, February 27, 1993, the most famous stretch of pavement west of Wall Street was closed to traffic and lined from one end to the other (some three city blocks) with more than 125 Ferraris, dating from 1948 to 1993. It was without question one of the most singularly impressive displays of Ferraris ever assembled. All for the introduction of Ferrari's 348 Spider.

The public debut of the new Ferrari was conducted by designer Sergio Pininfarina and Ferrari S.p.A. chairman and CEO Luca Cordero Di Montezemolo, who told the crowd of spectators that Ferrari chose Beverly Hills and Rodeo Drive for the car's world introduction because California is very important to Ferrari. (California represents some 35 percent of Ferrari's American market.)

Designer Sergio Pininfarina says that creating a new design is not an easy task, "The fundamental problem that exists with any new design is always the same. Our cars have been the best or among the best in the world, the highest prestige for 50 years. Every new car then is a challenge, because each time we have to reaffirm that we are good enough to redesign a car which brings such satisfaction to the owner."

Considering all of the designs he has created for Ferrari over the past 46 years, Pininfarina says, "It is difficult to say which one is the best because there are so many different designs, so many different types of cars." He thinks for a moment and as a smile comes across his face he says, "Yes, there is the Superamerica, which used to be my father's car, this is something unique, a Ferrari between the Ferraris, something extremely refined, extremely good taste, extremely powerful," and with a hint of humor in his voice he adds, "extremely expensive. The Superamerica is a car which is very dear to my heart."

The F 355, in either Berlinetta or Spider form, is the most powerful Ferrari ever produced with a naturally aspirated V-8 engine. Output from the 90-degree, 3.5-liter, 40-valve dohc V-8 is 375 hp at 8,250 rpm. Exhilarating performance is tempered by sophisticated computer-controlled, fully independent suspension, antilock disc brakes, and variable ratio power steering.

The F 355 Berlinetta and Spider have one of the most luxurious leather interiors ever designed for a Ferrari. A true driver's car, the layout is straightforward in design with the traditional Ferrari polished-steel shift gate.

The latest generation of Ferraris, beginning with the F40, have really become the signature cars for Sergio Pininfarina. "I have had the pleasure of meeting many people at the Concours, [Pininfarina is a judge each year at the Pebble Beach Concours d'Elegance] and they tell me that they own a new Ferrari, or an old one, and then they say, 'Thank you for what you have done.' There is no satisfaction in the world better to me than this."

His feelings about Ferrari, he says, are difficult to describe in Italian, impossible in English. "When I see all these red cars in the sunshine, I see one lifetime of work. In one way I feel very proud, and in another, very conscious of the importance of my position with Ferrari for the future."

That future has taken the form of the 456 GT 2+2, F 355 Berlinetta and Spider, and the F 50. With the debut of the 550 Maranello for 1997, and Ferrari has closed the circle giving the firm a new car in every V-8 and V-12 category from berlinetta and spider to GT 2+2, thus marking the beginning of Ferrari's second half-century. Cars, that however different from those built 50 years ago, still turn heads and set minds to dreaming.

Next
The Testarossa has become one of Ferrari's most successful models with a production run lasting from 1985 to 1996. From Testarossa, to 512 TR, to F 512 M, this body style is unsurpassed as the benchmark design of the 1980s.

The Testarossa's new flat-12 engine looked very much like the 512 BBi, but in fact was completely new and had no parts in common with its predecessor. Output from the 4942-cc, dohc, 48-valve engine was 390 hp at 6,300 rpm.

The 1995 Ferrari 456 GT 2+2 takes up where the 400i and 412 left off a decade earlier, offering Ferrari owners a luxurious four-passenger touring car built in the Ferrari tradition. The car features a clean-sheet-of-paper, 442-hp V-12, six-speed transmission, electronically actuated, fully independent suspension, and state-of-the-art traction control and antilock braking.

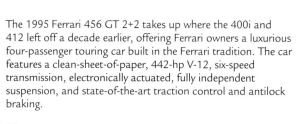

Track Testing Ferrari's Incredible F50

"HOW FAST?" The words blew back into my mouth as I tried to shout over the roar of wind surging past my head.

"ONE-SIXTY-FIVE!" Paul yelled. "I can do 180 on the next lap, but we'll have to go into turn one pretty hot. . . ."

"That's all right," I shouted, "I'll take your word for it. One-sixty-five is good enough."

Back in the pits, I realized that it wasn't the speed of the Ferrari F50 that had so impressed me—the car will break 200 mph if you give it enough room, but so will others—instead it was the undaunting way in which it tackled corners, as though inertia no longer had any relevance. More than the engine or body, it is the suspension that sets this Ferrari apart from other high-performance exotic sports cars. That, and a price of $480,000.

Few of Ferrari's vintage models can command that kind of money today, but after ever so little time in the F50 you understand why owners are willing to mortgage their souls to Modena for the privilege of leasing one.

"The lease," explains owner Paul Frame, "is Ferrari's way of preventing the market speculation that drove up the prices on F40s." Indeed, Ferrari is controlling the sale of the F50 by signing each owner to a two-year lease. "That's about $240,000 down and $5,500 a month," explains Frame. "Afterward, you have the option to buy the car for an additional $150,000." With owners locked into a two-year lease, there is little chance of speculators buying cars to resell. It is hoped the lease is worded to forbid subletting.

Money aside, this is the most remarkable nonracing car Ferrari has ever produced, although the line between race and road car in this case is so fine as to be almost imperceptible. The F50 is a street-legal Formula 1 car with a plush interior, as close to a purebred racer as any road car Modena has produced in the last half century. The F50 is the accumulation of 45 racing models and endless Granturismo and Sports models.

In theory, under the exotic Pininfarina-designed body, the F50 is a road-going adaptation of the 1990 Ferrari 641/2 Formula 1 car. It is built like a race car, around a central monocoque.

Made entirely of Cytec Aerospace carbon fiber, the F50 chassis weighs only 225 pounds and forms the central part of the car where the driver sits. Following Formula 1 design disciplines, the engine-gearbox-differential assembly is attached to the chassis with the engine anchoring the suspension, rear bumper, and bodywork elements. This is the first occasion that this system employing the engine as a structural element, as well as the propulsion medium, has been used on a street vehicle.

The F50's design places 43 percent of the car's weight on the front axles and 57 percent over the rear. To guarantee a tendency to understeer, the front track is 18 mm wider than the rear.

Prior to our track test, Frame ran the car at Texas World Speedway and attained 188.5 mph on the straight-away. "It's got really good gearing. The engine has a lot of torque in low rpm and one of the nice things about it is that it's streetable." Under 4,500 rpm the engine noise is muted. Get into the power over 4,500 revs and the F50 trumpets like a John Barry score. The engine actually changes temperament above 4,500 rpm and the two-stage induction system opens fully to double the volume of air being delivered. At the same time, the Motronic control unit reduces back pressure on the exhaust.

Frame admits that he hasn't really pushed the F50 that hard on the track. "I'm used to driving my F 355 Challenge

The styling of Ferrari's fiftieth anniversary model, the F50, is the most futuristic in the company's history. The Pininfarina body design is a road car adaptation of a Formula 1 race car.

When you settle into the driver's seat, you face an empty instrument pod until the power is switched on. Instrumentation is based on Formula 1 design and uses an 8-bit microprocessor that incorporates a downloadable event memory. The displays, which can only be seen by the driver, are LCD with 130 elements, transparency lit by electro-luminescent bulbs. The major gauges in analog display are the tachometer and speedometer, which overlap each other so that redline appears almost to the immediate top left of the speedometer. A panel of tell-tales is positioned to the left of the tach, using ideograms to indicate various warnings. Fuel gauge, lighting indicators, and a digital clock are inset along the bottom edge of the instrument display. The dash is completely finished in suede to reduce glare in the highly curved windshield.

The heart of every Ferrari since day one has been the engine. Here Formula 1 regulations again played a role in the design of the F50's 286.7-ci V-12. The layout is a narrow vee of 65 degrees based on Ferrari's 1990 F1 car but increased in displacement from 3.5 liters to 4.7 liters. Utilizing four overhead camshafts and five vales per cylinder (three intake, two exhaust—a total of 60 valves in case you're counting), bore and stroke is 3.35x2.72 inches and compression a healthy 11.3:1. As rated by Ferrari, maximum horsepower is 513 at 8,500 rpm. Peak torque, 347 ft-lb, is delivered at 6,500 rpm. And with an overall weight of just 2,712 lb dry, the F50 carries around a mere 5.3 lb per horsepower.

Car on slicks, so when I'm on street tires with the F50 I'm just a little tentative." It's hard to think of 188.5 mph as "tentative." Frame has already gone through one set of the specially designed Fiorano tires. Named after Ferrari's test track, they were developed by Goodyear and are an impressive 245/35ZR18 front and 355/30ZR18 rear.

"There is some talk about manufacturing an F50 *competizione*. If they do that, I'm sure someone is going to make some slicks, and then I'll have an opportunity to see what the car can really do," says Frame. What it can do with the low-profile Fioranos is paste you into the seatback in a heartbeat. Zero-to-60 mph time is 3.7 seconds.

There is an unusually solid sound when the doors close, not the hollow thump you heard in the F40. The doors are upholstered and finely detailed. By comparison, the interior of the F50 is like a Rolls-Royce, and considerably more spacious than the F40's. Still, it is purely functional, the lower dash panel and most of the exposed interior surfaces are carbon fiber. The floor mats are rubber.

Racing-style seats using a composite frame are luxuriously upholstered in Connolly leather surrounding red fabric inserts for the seatback and cushion. The driver's seat and pedal rack are both adjustable to tailor the car to each owner.

With its clean, uncluttered interior layout, the most prominent feature is the center tunnel and shifter. The F50 gearbox is a wonderful blend of old and new. The high-tech carbon fiber shift knob and lever rest inches above a traditional polished-steel shift gate, linking the driver to a six-speed transmission with ZF twin cone synchronizers and a limited slip differential.

Technology at such a high price must come in an appropriate package, and Carrozzeria Pininfarina has pushed the envelope with the F50's styling. This is simply an outrageous-looking automobile. With the massive air ducts in the hood, wide oval grille, and integrated head-lights, when seen head on, the F50 almost appears to be grinning. At nearly half a million dollars a copy, and with every one of the 349 cars to be built through 1997 already presold, someone certainly is.

The 1997 550 Maranello replaces the F 512 M as Ferrari's performance flagship. The new SWB Berlinetta is the first front-engined V 12 since the 365 GTB/4 Daytona. It is built on a 98.4-inch wheelbase chassis and uses independent front and rear suspension with computer-controlled damping, as on the F50. A dual-mode ASR (traction control) system prevents wheel spin, although it can be switched off by the driver.

With the debut of a replacement for the F 512 M (Testarossa), Ferrari has closed the circle giving the firm a new car in every V-8 and V-12 category from Berlinetta and Spider to GT 2+2, thus marking the beginning of Ferrari's second half century.

Index

Alfa Romeo, 9
Ascari, Alberto, 16, 19
Auto Avio Costruzione, 9
Balma, Angelo, 23
Bizzarrini, Giotto, 35, 37
Boano, Mario, 26
Bonami, Roberto, 21
Boxer engine, 73
Bracco, Giovanni, 34
Carrozzeria Pinin Farina, 18, 20, 23, 26, 30, 33
Carrozzeria Pininfarina, 37, 50, 67, 69, 80
Carrozzeria Scaglietti, 23, 37
Carrozzeria Touring, 12, 13
Carrozzeria Vignale, 17, 19, 20
Chinetti, Jr., Luigi, 64
Chinetti, Luigi, 10, 12, 16, 18, 19, 23–25, 39, 40, 41, 54–57, 65, 67
Chiti, Carlo, 35
Cisitalia, 24
Colombo, Gioacchino, 10
Farina, Battista "Pinin," 18, 24, 26
Ferrari, Dino, 61
Ferrari, Enzo, 9–11
Forghieri, Mauro, 35
Grossman, Bob, 41
Hoffman, Max, 24
Jano, Vittorio, 60
Lucas, Jean, 55
McQueen, Steve, 65
Michelotti, Giovanni, 23, 26
Models
    166 Barchetta competizione, 13
    166 Barchetta lusso, 13, 16
    166 Spyder Corsa, 10, 12
    166 MM Touring Barchetta, 13-16
    206 GT Dino, 60, 61

212, 17
212 Berlinetta, 18
212 Export, 19
212 Inter, 19, 20
225 Sport, 9, 11, 20, 21
250 GT Berlinetta "Tour de France", 32, 35
250 GT Berlinetta Lusso, 42–47
250 GT 2+2, 39
250 GT PF, 35
250 GT Spyder California Cabriolet Series I, 42
250 GT Spyder California Cabriolet Series II, 42
250 GT Spyder California, 40, 43
250 GT SWB Berlinetta, 33–37
250 GT SWB Competition, 37
250 GTO, 23
250 MM, 30, 31, 34
250 S, 34
265 GTB/C, 53, 58-59
275 GTB. 53-57
275 GTB/4 Berlinetta, 53, 54, 67
275 GTB/4 Spyder, 65, 67
275 GTB/4, 56, 67
275 GTB/4 (NART Spyder), 64–67
308 GTB, 74
308 GTBi, 77
308 GTS, 74
308GTB Qv, 77
328 Berlinetta, 77
328 GT Berlinetta, 78
328 GT Spyder, 79
328 Spyder, 77
330 GTC, 46, 50
330 GTS, 50, 51
340 America, 24, 25
342 America, 25

348 Spyder, 82
365 GT4 BB, 73
365 GTB/4 Berlinetta, 66, 71
365 GTB/4 Daytona, 67, 70, 71
365 GTB/4 Spyder, 69–71
365 GTS/4 Spyder, 66
375 America, 25
375 GTB/4 Berlinetta, 70
400 Superamerica, 39, 47
400 GT, 74
410 Superamerica, 24, 26, 28, 30, 31, 33, 39
456 GT 2+2, 82, 87, 90
500 Superfast, 39, 47–50
512 BB, 74, 77
512 TR, 80, 82, 88-90
550 Maranello, 82, 87, 95
815, 10
Daytona Spyder, 66
F 355, 82, 84-87
F 512 M, 82, 86
F40, 73, 77, 80
F50, 92, 93
Superfast I, 34
Moss, Stirling, 37
North American Racing Team (NART), 41, 56, 57
Pininfarina, Sergio, 28, 43, 54, 67
Savonuzzi, Mario, 26
Scaglietti, Sergio, 64
Scuderia Ferrari, 9, 56
Serafini, Dorino, 16
Stabilimenti Farina, 13, 16, 26
Taruffi, Piero, 9, 19, 55
Tavano, Ferdinand, 41
Villoresi, Luigi, 16, 19
von Neumann, John, 40